# The Moment

*there's no place like now*

David W. Jones

Adapted 2019 (The order for Sections two and three were switched.)

## The Moment

*seventy-five practices and praxises*
*for individuals and communities*
*living every moment as The Moment*
*taking church out of the past and into the present*
*out of sanctuaries and into homes, bars, and lives*
*for worship anywhere, anytime, and with anyone*
*everytime, everywhere, and with everyone*
*encountering God at any moment.*

Bible references are from The New Revised Standard Version unless otherwise noted.

# Contents

# SECTION ONE:
# What is a Moment?

*Yesterday is gone.*
*Tomorrow has not yet come.*
*We have only today.*
*Let us begin.*

Mother Teresa

# First Moments

Chicken Church began on the Britt's farm just outside Nashville. We started meeting regularly for worship followed by a meal together. One evening, while Etta was closing our time in prayer, a cackling hen came up behind her. I thought she was scatting like Ella Fitzgerald or speaking in tongues like a Pentecostal. The birds spoke so frequently at our gatherings on the farm, we referred to our time together as, "Chicken Church."

We have since met on other farms, in homes, in a bar, in churches, with other churches, and at a homeless shelter. Because "Chicken Church" sounds like fowl idolatry, we needed a new name. In one of my less than enlightened ideas, I wanted to call our worship services, *555*. I thought we might meet at 5:55. I envisioned *555* bumper stickers. They would be like the marathon *26.2* stickers but twenty times greater. Even if people could not figure out what the number meant, it might nurture curiosity. At least people would assume that we are all in extremely good shape. Our leadership team, Etta, Bob, and Carrie, all challenged me, "We don't know how to tell people what that is." I was also told that *555* sounded a lot like *666*.

After some discussion, the name, "The Moment" seemed to fit. It also had a nice sound to it, "Welcome to The Moment." Once we decided on, "The Moment," people wanted to know, "What is it?"

I replied, "I don't know, what do you think it is?" I hoped for insightful and life enriching discussions, but I got little or no response. Etta told me, "People don't know what to do with you when you say you don't know what The Moment is." Apparently, the Socratic method of answering a question with a question is dead.

When people asked, "What is The Moment?" I tried answering, "A new church." The response was enthusiastic, "Great!" but also provided no further conversation. People seem to know what 'church' is, and so they felt no need to talk about it anymore.

Hoping for more discussion and interaction, I tried a different response to, "What is The Moment?" I answered, "A new religion."

Again, to my disappointment, there were no conversations here either. People didn't say, "Great!" They did not say anything. Their eyes however were quite clear as they communicated, "You're going to hell."

Even more frustrating for many besides our lack of definition was that we did not have a set location. By definition, without a building, you are not a church as the dictionary declares that a *church* is a *building where religious services are held.*

When I met with some of my minister friends, they wanted to know where we were meeting. When I answered, "For a while, we're going to be..." They thought about it briefly, then said, "No, really, where will 'the church' be?" They had little imagination or vision of church without an address or a space. I understand. It is what we've always been taught going back to our childhood days of Sunday School with flannel boards and, "Here's the church, here's the steeple, open the door and see all the people."

# Minutes as Money

My father taught me the proverb, "Time is money," though not until my teenage years did I begin to understand what it meant. In my family, at  the age of sixteen, my brother, sisters, and I got jobs at the textile mill during our summer vacations from school. At $4.72/hour, well above minimum wage in those days, I converted all prices before spending any money to the time it took me to earn it calculating every expense to the quarter of an hour. I could tell you how much time I had to work to buy tickets to a movie, with or without a date, popcorn, or a drink.

As I got older, I learned that time was money and money was space. Getting married, after five years of apartment living, Carrie and I wanted to have our own home, a space for ourselves and for our potential children. The bank was willing to loan us money for a price, and we began transferring our time and money into a quantifiable and financial value measured in price-per-square-foot space. While my father taught me, "Time is money," the bank, with its thirty-year mortgage, showed me, "Life is space."

## The Dream of Fields and Buildings

My first church job was part-time at age nineteen. I watched the church plan, fundraise, and construct a Family Life Center. About the same time *The Field of Dreams* opened in theaters, a prophetic voice moved across the country through the churches promising, "If you build it, they will come."

My first fulltime position was in Georgetown, South Carolina. They already had a Family Life Center. The principle purpose for the center was to bring families into the church drawn by such an attractive facility. The gym did not bring in new members, what it did draw in was a crowd of people to play basketball. On one men's night, I asked a regular, "Mike, you are here two nights every week, why don't you come on Sunday morning?"

Mike replied, "You play basketball on Sunday morning?"

The second church I served struggled with interest on a long-term mortgage and a huge sanctuary used for one worship service per week.

Serving my third church, three weeks after I started my job, the head of the pastor search committee came into my office and asked, "When can we talk about the building renovation and new addition?" Because the church is by a river and in the hundred-year flood plain, it took us seven plans to meet local codes. Just after we renovated, the church flooded (see note on flood plain above) and then we renovated again. For the congregation's two hundredth anniversary, we published a history of the church, which reads largely as a life cycle of the buildings. Upon reflection, so has my own biography as I have invested a high percentage of my professional and personal life maintaining, keeping open, running, safeguarding, renovating, planning, and raising revenue for buildings and spaces.

When we started meeting in The Moment, I wanted to try church unlimited by space and time slots, worshipping anywhere and anytime, everywhere and every time. Besides, with our initial label of, "Chicken Church," if we would construct a building, it likely would look like this church in Florida.

## Moments Out of Space

*It's not a church if it's just got a steeple.*
*Just look inside – it's all about people.*
Paul Thorn

Trying to think of church and life as more than spaces, I stepped out of the sanctuary and into the synagogue. I read several books by Rabbi Abraham Joshua Heschel, which challenged me to start thinking in a more biblical and Christian understanding of time and space as well as the relationship between them. In *Between God and Man,* Rabbi Heschel challenged,

> *Technical civilization is (humanity's) conquest of space. It is a triumph frequently achieved by sacrificing an essential ingredient of existence, namely, time. In technical civilization, we expend time to gain space. To enhance our power in the world of space is our main objective. Yet to have more does not mean*

*to be more. The power we attain in the world of space terminates abruptly at the borderline of time. But time is the heart of existence.*

*To gain control of the world of space is certainly one of our tasks. The danger begins when in gaining power in the realm of space we forfeit all aspirations in the realm of time. There is a realm of time where the goal is not to have but to be, not to own but to give, not to control but to share, not to subdue but to be in accord. Life goes wrong when the control of space, the acquisition of things of space, becomes our sole concern.*

Rabbi Heschel began bringing me back from thinking of my life as space and to an understanding of the time of my life as space as I read in *The Sabbath,*

*Every one of us occupies a portion of space. He takes it up exclusively. The portion of space which my body occupies is taken up by myself in exclusion of anyone else. Yet, no one possesses time. There is no moment which I possess exclusively. This very moment belongs to all living (persons) as it belongs to me. We share time, we own space. Through my ownership of space, I am a rival of other beings; through my living in time, I am a contemporary of all other beings."*

After reading Rabbi Heschel's books, I started to see houses as spaces but being at home as my greater goal. I started looking for church beyond the limits of walls and spaces, even sacred spaces, and started expecting God in any space, any time, any location, and with any one – wherever and whenever God chooses.

## Moments Experiencing Time

*What year did Jesus think it was?*
George Carlin

A minute is sixty seconds and an hour is sixty minutes no matter where I am or what I am doing. However, my experience of sixty seconds or sixty minutes is quite different depending on where and how I am. If I am at home, in bed, asleep, sixty minutes seems like no time at all, but if I am outside on a cold night without enough clothing to keep me warm, then sixty minutes seems like much longer. There is the never changing measurement of time, but there is also how we experience it. We can't experience a minute, feel an inch, or taste a gram. They are all measurements. Albert Camus gives some simple ways to become aware of the difference between time experienced and time measured,

> *By spending one's days on an uneasy chair in a dentist's waiting-room; by remaining on one's balcony all of a Sunday afternoon; by listening to lectures in a language one doesn't know; by traveling by the longest and least-convenient train routes, and of course standing all the way; by lining up at the box-office of theaters and then not buying a seat; and so forth.*

Recognizing the difference between lifetime and the time of life is a huge step toward increasing our quality of life. For this wisdom, sages abound. Rory Sutherland is an advertising guru and an expert in types of time. Rory's group and a group of engineers were asked to improve the train ride from London to Paris, which takes about six hours. The engineers met and came up with a plan to build new and improved tracks from London to the coast at a cost of over nine billion dollars. Rory did not focus on the time of the ride but the experience of time on the ride. His solution was, "Hire all of the world's top male and female supermodels and pay them to walk the length of the train handing out free Chateau Petrus. After you pay for the super models and the red wine, you'd still have five billion dollars left, and people would ask for the trains to be slowed down."

The engineers were limited by an understanding of time only as something measured but not experienced. Rory understood them as two different types of time. He also understood that for most of us, just speeding up won't make our lives better.

Because the English language focuses largely on precise measurements, our understanding of time in English shows little distinction between minutes and moments. The dictionary reduces *moments* to *small or miniscule amounts of time.* The example of *moment* used in a sentence is, "I'll be there in a moment." In other words, "I'll be there very soon, in a matter of seconds." Like the definition of *church* that limits it to measureable boundaries as a *building where worship services are held,* so does our understanding of a *moment* as *a miniscule amount of time* confine it to minutes or seconds. To understand as well as live our moments, we have to think beyond our limiting dictionary definitions seeing moments as far more than minutes.

# Moments Encountering The Holy

Genesis 2: *Thus the heavens and the earth were finished, and all their multitude. ² And on the seventh day God finished the work that he had done, and he rested on the seventh day from all the work that he had done. ³ So God blessed the seventh day and hallowed it, because on it God rested from all the work that he had done in creation.*

Rabbi Heschel helped me again explore the limits of my understanding of time. In this excerpt from *The Sabbath*, he distinguishes between regular time and holy moments,

*One of the most distinguished words in the Bible is the word* kadosh *(קָדוֹשׁ), holy; a word which more than any other is representative of the mystery and majesty of the divine. Now what was the first holy object in the history of the world? Was it a mountain? Was it an altar?*

*It is, indeed, a unique occasion at which the distinguished word* kadosh *is used for the first time: in the Book of Genesis at the end of the story of creation. How extremely significant is the fact that it is applied to time: "And God blessed the seventh day and made it holy." There is no reference in the record of creation to any object in space that would be endowed with the quality of holiness.*

*This is a radical departure from accustomed religious thinking. The mythical mind would*

*expect that, after heaven and earth have been established, God would create a holy place--a holy mountain or a holy spring--whereupon a sanctuary is to be established. Yet it seems as if to the Bible it is holiness in time, the Sabbath, which comes first.*

*When history began, there was only one holiness in the world, holiness in time...*

## Moments Touching Eternity

Greek, like Hebrew, has a broader understanding of time than English. The Greeks had two different words for time, *Chronos* (χρόνος) and *Kairos.* (καιρός). Author Sarah Breathnach in *Simple Abundance*, gives clear insight to these two very different types of time and how we experience them.

*Chronos is clocks, deadlines, watches, calendars, agendas, planners, schedules, beepers. Chronos is time at her worst. Chronos keeps track... Chronos is the world's time. Kairos is transcendence, infinity, reverence, joy, passion, love, the Sacred. Kairos is intimacy with the Real. Kairos is time at her best. ...Kairos is Spirit's time. We exist in chronos. We long for kairos. That's our duality. Chronos requires speed so that it won't be wasted. Kairos requires space so that it might be savored. We do in chronos. In kairos we're allowed to be ... It takes only a moment to cross over from chronos into kairos, but it does take a moment. All that kairos asks is our willingness to stop running long enough to hear the music of the spheres.*

The ability to see the difference between *Chronos* and *Kairos*, *Kadosh* and regular time, moments and minutes, is so important I encourage you to read those passages again and pay attention to your experiences of both types of time. If you feel rushed, like an athlete with the ball while the clock ticks away with time running out, or if you feel an even greater anxiety, like Dorothy in the Wizard of Oz, and you are watching the sands of your life's hourglass fade away, then you are experiencing *chronos*. Not only are you experiencing it, you are controlled by it. If you feel alive, free from worry, time is your doorway to a greater reality, free from what might be to simply be present in what is, then you are experiencing *kairos*. T.S. Eliot wrote of life experienced in *kairos* when he wrote touching eternity,

> *Not the intense moment*
> *Isolated, with no before and after,*
> *But a lifetime burning in every moment.*

Time as a space, as a noun, as a commodity can never reach the fullness of time beyond space, beyond nouns to verbs, beyond buying and selling to living and loving as Henry Van Dykes noted,

> *Time is too slow for those who wait, too swift for those who fear, too long for those who grieve, too short for those who rejoice; but for those who love, time is eternity.*

# Moments Beyond The Terror of Time

Matthew 6: *25 "Therefore I tell you, do not worry about your life, what you will eat or what you will drink, or about your body, what you will wear. Is not life more than food, and the body more than clothing?26 Look at the birds of the air; they neither sow nor reap nor gather into barns, and yet your heavenly Father feeds them. Are you not of more value than they? 27 And can any of you by worrying add a single hour to your span of life?*

Worrying can't add a single minute to our lives, but we will try! Jesus hits at the heart of our worrying when he asks, "Can any of you by worrying add a single hour to the span of your life?" He points us toward just how short our lives are when he refers to the length of life as a span – the measure between the tips of an average man's thumb and pinky. Life is so short when we measure it in months or minutes. When time is running out, it is hard to live in the present. Jesus points to not only our anxiety about the shortness of life, but also to where it comes from, our attempt to think  of life limited in terms of hours, minutes, seconds, or spans.

Minutes, hours, days, months are ways to measure what, at it's core, is not measureable – life. If we think in terms of measurements, then life is always running out, and ultimately, can be a terror of constant worry. We feel like Jim Morrison who said, "The future is uncertain but the end is always near."

In J.R.R. Tolkein's *The Hobbit,* tiny Bilbo Baggins leaves the comfort of home enticed by a wizard to participate in an adventurous journey. On his way, Bilbo gets lost deep inside a series of caves and can't find his way out. He encounters a once human creature who has aged without dying becoming more and more a monster over time. The creature's name had been forgotten as he was known for his single sound, a pathetic gasping of air, *Gol-lum.*

In desperation to find a way out, Bilbo makes a deal with the monster. If he can outsmart him in a battle of riddles, then Gollum will show him the way out, if not, then Gollum will eat him for dinner. Gollum asks,

> *This thing all things devours:*
> *Birds, beasts, trees, flower;*
> *Gnaws iron, bites steel;*
> *Grinds hard stones to meal;*
> *Slays king, ruins town,*
> *And beats high mountains down.*

Bilbo wondered what could devour all things including birds and beasts and trees and flowers, iron, steel, kings and mountains. Sensing that Bilbo didn't know the answer, Gollum started moving closer to him. Bilbo was frightened. He sensed his time to answer and his time to live were running out. He wanted to shout out, "Give me more time! Give me time!" but all that he could yell was, "Time! Time!" which, of course, was the answer.

*Time all things devours:*
*Birds, beasts, trees, flower;*
*Time gnaws iron, bites steel;*
*Grinds hard stones to meal;*
*Time slays king, ruins town,*
*And beats high mountains down.*

When we think in terms of time as measured in minutes or other units, time is always devouring. As the master of horror fiction Stephen King pointed out, "Time takes it all, whether you want it to or not." When all we understand or sense is time measured, minutes, hours, weeks, months, and years, then there is no greater monster than time as it devours all. We cry out like Bilbo, "Time! Time!" seeking more minutes but missing our moments in the process.

## Moments Are Only Now

*Happiness, not in another place but this place...not for another hour, but this hour.* Walt Whitman

One of the most moving of our worship experiences was at the Women's Shelter in Nashville. The congregation taught me to cherish each moment of my life as every moment is The Moment for every moment is *now*.

It was an unusually cold night, even for February, so the chapel at the women's shelter was packed. Etta began by turning the whole congregation into a choir. Danny Flowers told a little of his background and then sang, *I Was a Burden*, followed by Bob singing, *It's a Wonderful World,* which moved even the ever cool handed guitar player to a place of tears. When I came up to speak, I was introduced as pastor for The Moment. I felt that The Moment needed some description. I said something like this, "The Moment is now. It is here. Whatever was before, is not now. Your past, it's history. It's over. It is not now. This moment is now."

I realized that the teacher had become the student. For most of the congregations I have served, there is little distinction between the moments before worship and after. On cold winter days, they leave a warm home, get into a warm car, and come to a warm church. They were safe at home, safe in their car, and feel safe at church. For this congregation at the shelter, the particular moment was far different from what they had experienced earlier or what was ahead of them the next day. I spoke to them, and just as they had accepted the dinner prepared for them earlier, they gladly received what I had to offer in celebration of the particular moment we were entering together. I said, "If you were cold before, you are not now. If you were hungry before, you are not now. If you were unsafe before, you're safe now. We don't know what tomorrow will be. Worrying about it won't change it. We are here. We are together. This is the moment. This is now." They understood, "Now." Through their perspective, I was getting an education in "Now," as Eckhart Tolle wrote,

*Time isn't precious at all, because it is an illusion. What you perceive as precious is not time but the one point that is out of time: the Now. That is precious indeed. The more you are focused on*

*time—past and future—the more you miss the*
*Now, the most precious thing there is.*

## Moments Ending to Begin

*I can't talk to you in terms of time.*
*Your time and my time are different.*
Graham Greene

"Why do you hate Indians?" someone asked me after a sermon.

"What?" I asked.

"In the sermon, you said that you hate Indians."

"I heard it, too," said another person now entering the conversation.

"Look, I never said that…" I replied.

"Yes, you did," they replied in a chorus. "A lot," said the first. "I hate Indians. I hate Indians. You said it over and over." "Yes," the second agreed. "You talked about some long book, then just kept saying, 'I hate Indians.'"

"Wait a minute," I insisted. "I didn't say, 'I hate Indians.' I said, 'I hate endings.'"

"Oh," they replied. "That makes more sense."

I do hate endings. I read the unabridged version of *Les Miserable* by Victor Hugo. I stopped on page 1,086 with a little more than 100 pages to go. Not because I didn't like the story, I still do. It's one of my favorite novels. In fact, if my wife had been agreeable, Nathan's middle name would have been Valjean. Nathan Valjean Jones, after the main character in the book. When I started my own publishing company, I named it *Valjean Press.* I didn't stop on page 1,086 because I was at a boring place in the novel. I stopped on page 1,086 because I hate endings. I hate endings so much that I hesitate to eat the last bite of an ice cream cone, drink the last drop of a milk shake, or chew the last piece of gum. I grieve over their finality, sorry that they are over. I hate endings so much that I don't like to say, "Goodbye." "Goodbye is too final." On the telephone, instead of goodbye, I say, "Talk to you later," or "Come see us," "See you soon." To a person in front of me, instead of goodbye, I say, "Take care," "Drive carefully," or, "See you later." If I say, "Goodbye," it is usually short and quick, "bye." Not a real goodbye, just a 'bye' that is short for "bye for now." Goodbyes are too final.

Moments help me come to terms with endings. When minutes run out, the game is over. When a moment ends, a new moment can begin. Minutes are based on a linear understanding of time. When life is lived in calendars, minutes expiring, endings are final. Relationships end. Jobs end. People end. I end. Caught in minutes, I see endings and only endings.

Moments are different. Moments end like seasons with a new beginning to follow like Spring ends with Summer's beginning. Sometimes the endings are so fluid that it is hard to notice when one stopped and another started. Moments end, but the ending is never final. Moments point to a cycle of beginning, end, and new beginning. The closing door of one moment is the opening of another. The challenge is to move from one moment to the next, to let go of the past to enter the present.

As a reminder of the nonfinality of endings, the early church chose Sunday as its Sabbath instead of Saturday to celebrate Jesus' resurrection. Easter was not a celebration once a year but weekly reorientations to

25

God's way of bringing new beginnings from even horrifying endings.

For those who live moments, the letting go of one season is the requirement for moving to the next. Moments require letting go and receiving. Simple steps; often quite difficult.

## Moments Larger than Death

A few years ago, the day after Christmas, we were with friends at their home. Santa had brought them two sparkling new four-wheelers. James and I went to test them out. Because we were just going for a little spin, we didn't wear helmets. (In literature, we call this foreshadowing.)

James started ascending a large mountainous hill through the trees. I didn't want to follow directly behind him because if he got stuck, I was well aware I couldn't back a four wheeler down a mountain. I set out blazing my own trail, determined to get to the top before James. The race was on (whether James knew it or not).

When the front end popped up the first time, hitting a root, I didn't think too much of it, but when I hit a log on the incline, I took notice. I took notice because I was thrown backward, off the four-wheeler, spinning down the hill, shoulder over shoulder. As I tumbled, in my flash views of uphill, downhill, and dirt, I noticed the four-wheeler was coming down the hill, at me, end over end.

Time slowed down. I'm sure the clocks didn't change their ticking, but in some way, mentally or otherwise, I transcended time. I even transcended my body. My body was spinning, but my mind was calm, focused, and contemplating. As my body turned shoulder over shoulder and I rolled downward, I had a personal conversation with myself and explored my situation. I thought, 'Self, I wonder if I can survive if that four-wheeler rolls over me.'

Self replied, 'Probably not, especially if it rolls over your head. You better get moving.'

I replied, 'Moving? Have you noticed I am rolling down a hill?'

Self replied, 'I don't care. Have you noticed the four-wheeler coming at you? You better tell yourlegs to get going.'

I stepped upward and got back to my feet and into time, which then returned to its normal second by second pace. I stood and watched the four-wheeler roll end over end three more times down the hill. I did a self-check. I could feel my heart pounding and beating faster than its usual cadence. Nothing seemed broken or even injured outside of a little throbbing in my head.

James returned, looked at me, and looked at the four-wheeler upside down at the bottom of the hill. "You wrecked Emily's four-wheeler," he said.

I smiled, raised both arms as if I'd just won the Tour de France or an Olympic Medal. "I'm alive!" I declared waiting for the national anthem.

That was a moment. Not a space in time but a transcendence of time. A movement beyond what was for something else. I had emotions, but didn't become them. I had thoughts, but wasn't dominated by them. I was still, even though my body was rolling down a hill chased by a tumbling four-wheeler. I understand you might say, "It was just a few seconds." Yes, if you could measure it, but it was also not limited to seconds. It was beyond seconds, other than tick or tock. I touched eternity.

In Mark 8, Matthew 16, and Luke 17 Jesus advises, "If you want to save your life, you'll lose it, but if you lose your life, you'll find it." Almost losing my life that Christmas gifted me with a year full of moments. For the next twelve months, I had one of the best years of my life. Everything seemed to fall into perspective. I could have died. They could have come and carried my crushed skull and body away. Instead, I walked away with scratches, a small amount of blood, and an irrelevant repair bill for a four-wheeler.

The perspective I got was beyond minutes. I lost my hurried sense of *chronos* and time running out because my time could have already run out. My life wasn't expiring but instead this was all bonus, all extra, like winning a free game of pinball or ski ball or whatever people play in the remaining arcades. All was, as they say in my home state of South Carolina, "Gravy." Every encounter was a gift and not something to save since everything I had and was could have been lost. I had more and more moments, transcending time. I started to understand that living in the present wasn't hedonistic but mindful. Whether enjoying each spoonful of a bowl of ice cream or just being shoulder to shoulder with my wife or children watching television, almost dying made me more alive.

As time has gone on and my life is distant from that particular nearly dead experience, I have returned to former patterns of cramming my minutes with more activity and experiencing fewer of the moments of my life, but I remember the difference between minutes and moments. From that almost tragic accident, I have rewritten Henry Van Dykes words adapting them to my own experience.

> *Time is too slow for those who wait, too swift for those who fear, too long for those who grieve, too short for those who rejoice; but for those who love (and those who walked away from a four-wheeler tumbling end over end at their heads), time is eternity.*

## Moment Review

*Forever is composed of nows.*
Emily Dickinson

We ask so often, "What time is it?" when the more important question for life is, "What kind of time is it?" Is it minutes or moments?

Minutes are measurements of time.

Moments are experiences that transcend time.

Minutes are time at its worst.

Moments are life at its fullest.

Minutes are measured, clocked, labeled, scheduled, ordered, alarmed, hurried, packed, and expiring. Minutes tell us when to wake, when to eat, when to leave, what to do, when to return, and when to sleep. Minutes plot our lives in a tangible and visible grid on paper, calendars, schedules, computers, and mobile phones. Minutes are the thin train tracks of our lives with a clear beginning at birth when we get on board and a final stop when exiting is required. When we are young, minutes put life out of reach in some far away future telling us, "Not yet, but maybe one day." When we are older, minutes count downward like the scoreboard in a basketball game visibly reminding us that our, "Time is running out," and that, "What Once Was" is far more than "What's Left."

All that minutes are: measurable, numerable, ordered, scheduled, alarmed, and expiring, moments are not. While minutes are about the quantity of life, moments are about the quality of life and deny quantification. Moments are other. Moments transcend charting, calculating, and ordering. Moments are life beyond minutes. Time may be repeated. The same minute will occur tomorrow, but moments are always singular, distinct, particular, and unique. Every moment is a new moment. Every moment is a fresh moment. Every moment is a first moment with new possibilities, new realities, and new life beyond limits of scale, schedule, or measurement. In every moment, you are born all over again, resurrected from what was to what is for moments can be holy, touch eternity, never ticking away but ending to begin. Moments are larger than life or death, far more than minutes, for moments are now.

# SECTION TWO:
# Moment Praxis

*For apart from inquiry, apart from the praxis, individuals cannot be truly human. Knowledge emerges only through invention and re-invention, through the restless, impatient, continuing, hopeful inquiry human beings pursue in the world, with the world, and with each other.* Paulo Freire

# Orthoducksy

*The knowledge of God is very far from the love of God.*
Pascal

When we started meeting together for The Moment, the two questions we faced were, "Who are we?" and "What do we do?" Those questions weren't unique to us but rooted in a debate that has gone on for thousands of years and across continents. Each question represents a distinct approach to life. Like all good paradigms, each has its own fancy Latin word.

*Orthodoxy,* or *right thought,* assumes that thinking comes before action, and if you think the right thoughts, accept the correct precepts, then you'll make the right choices and do what is right. The application within the church is – believe in Christ and you'll act like Christ.

*Orthopraxis,* or *right practice,* asserts that action precedes thinking, and if you do the right actions then you will think the right thoughts, and what's more, you'll become who you are trying to become. The application in the church is – act like Christ and not only will you believe, you will become Christ-like.

Which of the two has greater results? Soren Kierkegaard shared his observation in the following story, which I've embellished. If you share it with a group, make sure and have them shout, "Amen!" where appropriate.

*The First Marshland Church for Ducks was having its Easter service, and birds traveled from far away packing the sanctuary with wall to wall down. They sang their favorite hymns, "On the*

33

*Wings of a Snow White Duck," "For the Beauty of the Marsh," and "Faith of Our Waddlers"*

*The duck preacher took his stand behind the podium. "My brother and sister ducks," he began. "Look around you at those next to you. Look at yourself. God has given us beautiful feathers."*

*"Amen!" the congregation quacked.*

*"God has given us beautiful feathers for a purpose."*

*"Amen!"*

*"God has given us beautiful feathers so we could fly."*

*"Amen!"*

*"God has given us beautiful feathers so we could sail high above the clouds."*

*"Amen!"*

*"God has given us beautiful feathers so we could soar on wings like eagles."*

*"Amen!"*

*The minister went on and on for a half an hour preaching about God's gift of flight. Louder and louder the congregation shouted back "Amen!" after "Amen!" However, when the service was over, every one of those ducks waddled home.*

Orthodoxy, right thought hoping for right action, is not only ineffective, it can turn even the most committed people into spectators, like the ducks in Kierkegaard's story. However, orthopraxis, right action leading to right thinking can not only transform individuals but so much more. Praxis is the becoming way.

# Praxis: Becoming Patient, Kind, and More

Psychologist William James called Praxis the "as if" principle. Shakespeare wrote about praxis when he penned, "Assume a virtue if you have it not." Father Richard Rohr affirmed the power of praxis over orthodoxy when he observed, "We do not think ourselves into new ways of living. We live ourselves into new ways of thinking."

Praxis is simply this, if you wish to possess a quality or an emotion, act "as if" you already had it, let it get hold of you, and it will. If you want to be patient, act like you are, and you will be. If you want to be kind, act like you are, and you will be. If you want to be compassionate, act like you are, and you will be. Enact a virtue to become the virtue. Twelve Step groups call this, "Faking it until you make it." If you want to not drink, act like you don't. If you want to become sober, act like you already are. Fake it long enough, and you'll become what you enact as long as becoming is your goal. If your hope is to simply hide your secrets, hoping others will think differently of you, then it's not praxis. Jesus referred to many of the religious in his day as "hypocrites," a term which came from the theater meaning "actors." These religious people, mostly leaders, were not enacting to become, they were simply acting as if they were already, but Jesus knew better.

Praxis can affect not just who you are becoming but how you feel. You can not only praxis your way into a virtue but the feelings that accompany it. Tony Campolo tells this story as an example.

*A man went to see a counselor about his marriage. "I'm not in love with my wife any longer. What can I do?"*

*The counselor replied, "First make a list of ten things you would do if you were in love. Second, do those things each day." The man found that by acting like a lover, in time he felt like a lover and fell in love all over again with his wife. His actions affected his feelings.*

*In love and relationships, there are seldom quick fixes. That was true in this case. Acting like a lover, the man didn't go straight home from work. He took a shower and put on a suit. He bought flowers. When he got home, he went to the front door and rang the doorbell, bouquet in hand. His wife opened the door and started crying. "What's wrong?" he asked.*

*"I've had a terrible day," she said. "First, Jimmy broke his arm. Second, the car wouldn't start. And now you come home drunk."*

## Praxis: Becoming an Athlete

Imagine a high school football team that has lost every game. A local team booster who happens to own a car dealership promises a new car to each player if they can win the last game of the season against their cross-town rivals. You know what would happen. Throughout the week, the team would practice hard. When the game came, the players would run onto the field ripping through the paper held by the cheerleaders as if it were, well, paper. They would jump up and down awaiting the kickoff. Then they would lose as they had every game prior. Motivation means little without training, practice, and becoming.

Imagine a University that hires a football coach who takes athletes into the locker room and every day, instead of drills, exercises, and practices, this coach only teaches the theory of the sport. He might even bring in the physics professors to talk about force and angle and proper blocking and tackling. When game time came, what would happen? How long would that coach's contract last?

Passion, theoretical discussion, and planning mean little if becoming is your goal, yet, go to church and tell me what you see? Is the focus on theory and passion or on practice, doing, and becoming?

Like the ducks in Kierkegaard's story, church can take participants and turn us into spectators. In athletics, only participants grow. I coached the same girls' soccer team for ten seasons. Without exception, if a player came to practice and games, worked a little on her own then she matured, became a better player and team member. Over those five years, I also observed one group that changed little at all. Intellectually they learned more about the game, but they did not develop in any observable way. Do you know which group that was? The parents. The parents never changed. Spectators don't. Even the way they yelled for (or sometimes at) their child didn't change.

Praxis helps us take our place on the field where growth and development are inevitable. No matter how awkward any sport is at the beginning, practice enough and the unnatural becomes natural, often without thought or reflection, and sometimes even without vision like in this example.

Michigan State Football Coach, Duffy Daugherty, told this story of Dave Kaiser's last second field goal which gave MSU a 17-14 victory over UCLA. As Kaiser came back to the bench to meet the roaring enthusiasm of his teammates, the Coach said, "Nice going, Dave, but I noticed you didn't watch the ball after you kicked it. How come?"

Kaiser replied, "You're right coach, I didn't watch the ball. I was watching the referee to see how he would call it. You see, I forgot my contact lenses. They are back at the hotel. I couldn't even see the goal posts. I needed the ref to know if I made the kick."

Daugherty was furious that Kaiser had not told him about his contacts, but after he thought it over he changed his mind. Why shouldn't his kicker boot it without seeing the whole field? He was a disciplined athlete and had practiced for years. He knew the angle and the distance from his position even though he could not see the goal posts. Through his years of practice, he had accomplished more than learning to kick, he had become a kicker with skill which he could apply in many different pressure filled situations, some of his own creating by leaving his contact lenses back at the hotel. That's praxis, practice in order to become, enabling not just knowledge but skill which becomes part of who and how you are, which you can apply in an infinite number of scenarios and situations, without overthinking.

Athletes understand becoming. They understand that no one learns a game over night no matter how much energy, passion, or thought you put into it. Becoming an athlete or a team takes discipline and practice which is why images of athletics are used again and again by writers in the Bible. For example,

1 Corinthians 9: *24 Do you not know that in a race the runners all compete, but only one receives the prize? Run in such a way that you may win it. 25 Athletes exercise self-control in all things; they do it to receive a perishable*  *wreath, but we an imperishable one.*

Hebrews 12: *1 Therefore, since we are surrounded by so great a cloud of witnesses, let us also lay aside every weight and the sin that clings so closely, and let us run with perseverance the race that is set before us...*

Hebrews 12: *11 Now, discipline always seems painful rather than pleasant at the time, but later it yields the peaceful fruit of righteousness to those who have been trained by it. 12 Therefore lift your drooping hands and strengthen your weak knees, 13 and make straight paths for your feet, so that what is lame may not be put out of joint, but rather be healed.*

1 Timothy 4: *Train yourself in godliness,* [8] *for, while physical training is of some value, godliness is valuable in every way, holding promise for both the present life and the life to come.*

## Praxis: Becoming Married

There is a great need for a praxis approach to relationships, especially marriage. Couples spend a lot of time focusing on coming down the aisle to get married as if marriage was a thing to acquire or a status to achieve in an instant. From an orthodoxy approach, if the minister, the couple, the congregation, and the state all affirm you are married then you must be. From an orthopraxis approach, married is something you continue to become all the days of your life requiring different skills in different stages.

I take a praxis approach in the personal words I offer to couples during their wedding ceremony. For me, in a marriage ceremony, there are more symbols than just the rings. My favorite to focus on is the clothes. Couples usually take far more time choosing their outfits than their vows. The most popular wedding passage is 1

Corinthians 13, but the second most popular is my favorite,

> Colossians 3: *²As God's chosen ones, holy and beloved, clothe yourselves with compassion, kindness, humility, meekness, and patience. ¹³ Bear with one another and, if anyone has a complaint against another, forgive each other; just as the Lord has forgiven you, so you also must forgive. ¹⁴ Above all, clothe yourselves with love, which binds everything together in perfect harmony.*

After I read this passage, I usually take some time and just have them 'be'. Weddings have so much put into them, the couple can move so fast through the service that they don't remember much of it later. I invite the couple to relax, breathe, pay attention to the details, look at the people, feel the presence of their friends and the congregation, and feel their support and prayers for them and their relationship. Then I ask them to face me as I offer some words of encouragement. Focusing on the clothes, I'll say something like this,

> *Here you are. You are dressed nicely. You will likely never dress this nicely again. When you chose your clothes for today, you didn't just go to your closet and get the best outfit you have. You went and got something better. These clothes are part of what you are promising to each other today. By standing here in these clothes, you are promising to give better than your best.*

*As a child, perhaps you played dress up, imagining what you might become a firefighter, a doctor, an astronaut, a trash truck driver. You put on the outfits of what you wanted to become. Today, you chose these clothes for a similar reason. You are promising to grow, to mature to become, promising to give to each other not just who you are, but who you can be.*

*When Paul said, "Clothe yourselves in love," Paul was challenging us to give each other better than our best. Love is something you may not be good at now, but dress up in it enough, and you will be. You will be better and better by putting on love so often that over time... you'll become loving. It's the same with patience. You may not be patient now, but put it on often enough and you will be. You may not be attentive now, but put it on often enough and you will be. To each other, this day, you are promising, "I'm dressed in clothes better than any I had because I'm not promising you my best, I'm promising better than my best. I'm promising you who I will become, promising who we can become, together. The clothes are part of the promise."*

That's praxis, clothe yourself with love and in time the clothes will make the man, and the clothes will make the woman, clothes will make the relationship. Clothe yourselves in love, and you will become loving.

The beauty of love in any relationship is that love is one of the few skills that can improve with age throughout your life. Anger is not that way, if you stay angry at someone for years, you are ill. Fear is not that way. If you stay afraid of bedroom closets throughout your life, you are childish. However, if you love someone for a lifetime, giving love the discipline, the determination, the training, and the practice that it takes, then you will become a masterful lover. As the old proverb says, "A great lover is not someone who can romance a different person every night, but a great lover is someone who can romance the same person for fifty years."

## Praxis: Becoming Mature

On a recent Saturday, I watched a movie for *Mature Audiences.* I'm interested in how this label, "Mature Audiences," is used. We say to children, "You can't watch this, it is for *Mature Audiences*." I want to call the people who came up with this name because I don't think they have a good understanding of "mature" or "adult." When I say, "Adult Film," what do you think of? Really? Don't go there.

The movie I watched was an old one, from 1952, *High Noon* with Gary Cooper and Grace Kelly. It had been advertised as an Adult Western. There was no nudity, no profanity, and very little shooting. There isn't a gun fight until the last fifteen minutes of the movie. So, why was it an adult film?

Pretty much everyone in it is stereotypical. The bad guys wear black. They scowl. They don't like each other.

They don't like their horses. They have their bad guy music. Villain music is full of *B's*. *Ba-ba-ba da - da – da – da. DUM.* Hero music, in contrast, has a lot of T's. *Ta-te-te ta tat a ta.*

The town's people are also stereotypical. They talk a lot but do little. They claim to support the Marshal, but they run in the end. The only characters with any depth are Marshal Will Kane (Gary Cooper) and Amy Fowler (Grace Kelly).

At the beginning of the movie, the bad guys are riding into town, *ba- ba- ba- da- da* while Will and Amy are getting married. After the wedding, Will, The Marshal, turns over his badge. Amy, his new wife, is a Quaker. She does not believe in violence. He is giving up being a Marshal out of respect for her, out of love for her. However, before they can run off, they get word that Frank Miller is coming back to town to join up with the three bad guys we've already seen. His train is due to arrive at High Noon.

The town goes into a nervous frenzy, "We need you Marshall." Will is conflicted but sensing it as his duty, he takes back his badge. Amy is furious and wants to leave him, but she is torn between her values and her love for him. Much of the movie is looking at the eyes of Will and Amy, Cooper and Kelly, and their struggle. Tough stuff, but it is adult stuff. It is an adult film. Two adults struggling with difficult choices in an immature world.

Perhaps more people should watch "Adult Films" like these. We suffer from a lack of maturity in leadership and a seeming unawareness to recognize maturity when we see it or notice its absence when we don't. We confuse maturity with age, as a place in time you arrive instead of a process throughout the times of your life. We tell our children a fairy tale when we say, "You can grow up and get a job," or "You can grow up and get married," or even, "You can grow up and have children." The implication is that there is a clear order to growing up, you do that first, then, as an adult, you get married. What we should say is, "You can get married and grow up." "You can get a job and grow up." "You can have children and grow up." If you do all these things and refuse to grow up, then it probably won't go well for you. The only places you can go with a refusal to grow up and be put in roles of leadership are in religion and politics.

In my last parish, I remember a resignation letter from a member and leader in the church. He explained that his family had come to the church years before because it was a lot closer to their house and much shorter drive. He wrote of how much they initially liked the church and how, for a long time, the church, "worked for them." He then went on to give a long list of reasons of why the church "no longer worked for them" and ended by encouraging others of the like-minded, who, if the church wasn't working for them, to follow his lead and leave.

I still feel the need to apologize. Somehow, I gave the message that church was a place that is ever supposed to "work for you." In all my significant relationships, especially my relationship with God, they more often work on me than work for me. I find great kinship in Genesis with the story of Jacob who comes away after wrestling with God all night, and like Jacob who limped the rest of his life, God often works me over as much as works on me. If we read the Bible in its raw nonpasteurized or nonpastorized version, it's very clear that neither God nor God incarnate work for people. God works on people. God loves all of us as we are, but God loves us too much to leave us that way in our flat lives when there is so much more we can become. More than a lack in morality, our culture, especially the church, suffer from a lack of maturity.

After an emotionally intense congregational meeting, a member of the church apologized to my son. "I'm sorry you had to see that," he said. "Sometimes adults act like children."

Nathan, then ten years old, was offended that the behavior of those adults would be associated with his age bracket and replied, "I'd never act like that." The immaturity of the adults offended my ten year old.

Poet Maya Angelou described our confusion over maturity,

*Most people don't grow up. Most people age. They find parking spaces, honor their credit cards, get married, have children, and call that maturity. What that is, is aging.*

The early church understood maturity was a necessity in the communal life. They did not see Jesus' frequent challenges to be childlike as permission to be childish and understood that to have a sensible morality a sensible maturity was required. Paul encouraged maturity frequently in his letters to congregations. He wrote,

1 Corinthians 13: [11] *When I was a child, I spoke like a child, I thought like a child, I reasoned like a child; when I became an adult, I put an end to childish ways.*

1 Corinthians 14: *²⁰ Brothers and sisters, do not be children in your thinking; rather, be infants in evil, but in thinking be adults.*

Ephesians 4: *¹⁴ We must no longer be children, tossed to and fro and blown about by every wind of doctrine, by people's trickery, by their craftiness in deceitful scheming. ¹⁵ But speaking the truth in love, we must grow up in every way into him who is the head, into Christ, ¹⁶ from whom the whole body, joined and knit together by every ligament with which it is equipped, as each part is working properly, promotes the body's growth in building itself up in love.*

## Praxis: Becoming Possible

*If I were to wish for anything, I should not wish for wealth and power, but for the passionate sense of the potential, for the eye which, ever young and ardent, sees the possible. Pleasure disappoints, possibility never. And what wine is so sparkling, what so fragrant, what so intoxicating, as possibility!* Soren Kierkegaard

About 400 years before Jesus, Plato taught the world about perfection in his Philosophy of Forms. According to Plato, everything in existence

was just a shadowy representation of a higher perfect form, like shadows on a cave wall represent the objects casting the image from the fire light. For everything there is a higher perfect form. The chair you are sitting in is merely a representation of a perfect chair. A horse is a representation of a perfect horse. Everything in existence has a higher perfect form.

Some 400 years later, when Jesus was born, Plato's ideas of perfection were still the dominant philosophy. God was perfect, righteous, holy, sinless, without flaw. Humanity was a dung heap compared to God. However, among life in the poop pile, some were less putrid than others. The religious in Jesus' day saw themselves as far from perfect, but in comparison, far more perfect than your regular run of the mill sinner. They were confident if the people of the world would all try and be more like them, the world would be a better place. In order to help others, they were glad to point out all the areas in which people had fallen short from the glory of God's perfect plan.

Today, The Platonic Model of Perfection is still followed religiously with each church believing that even though we are all sinners, some are just a little less sinful than others. In order to be helpful, like the other Platonic Perfectionists that have come before us, we don't begin by validating other people as beloved, we begin by invalidating others as far from perfect. We consider that the best way to be helpful.

The Platonic Model of Perfection is also primary in education, from the primary grades on up. If you take a test and answer 100 questions and answer accurately on 97 of them, your paper may be returned to you with a red, -3. Even if your test has a 97 on it, if asked, "How did you do?" you will likely answer, "I missed 3." Plato would be proud. We learn to grade ourselves on just how far from perfection we are always seeking that perfect Platonic form.

There is an alternative. For example, I heard of a teacher who started marking her tests differently. She got rid of her red marker. She put the number answered correctly on the paper. For a child who only got three correct, she put a *3* and a smiley face. The child asked her, "Why did you put a smiley face on my paper?"

She replied, "Because you got *3* right. If you got three, then you can get the rest."

She was not saying, "There is no goal, no scale, no measuring." What she is saying is, "Let's celebrate potential. You got three correct, that means you are capable of getting more."

Rather than showing what the child could not do, she pointed the child toward potential. Billy, in this next story needed a teacher like her, and parents, and pastors, and…

*A teacher asked her third grade class, "What do you want to be when you grow up?"*

*She got the standard answers, "Fireman. Doctor. Astronaut."*

*Then she asked the only child who had no response, "Billy, what do you want to be when you grow up?"*

*Billy replied, "Possible."*

*She did not understand, "Possible? What do you mean?"*

*He replied, "Everybody is always telling me, 'Billy, you're impossible. When I grow up, I want to be possible."*

Possibility or Potential is a contrasting model to Platonic Perfection and dates back to the same era as Plato. Plato had a student named, Aristotle. When Plato died, Aristotle was hoping to be appointed to Plato's position as a tenured professor of philosophy. When he didn't get the job, dejected, he left the city and went out into the forest to rethink his life. While he was out in the woods, he touched a tree.

Touching something alive, Aristotle thought how limited Plato's idea of 'perfection' was when it came to living things. What worked well in the classroom had little application with living things. What relevance did perfection have to do with trees, shrubs, flowers, birds, deer, or people? There was no 'perfect' form for anything alive. Living things come in so many varieties there can be no perfect form as each has a particularly unique and distinctive form of its own. Instead of perfection, Aristotle focused on 'potential'. He used the word, *telos.* In an acorn is the *telos* of an oak tree. In a tadpole is the *telos* of a frog. In a kitten is the *telos* of a cat. In a baby is the *telos* of an adult.

To the frustration of Jesus' adversaries, he was a *telos* man. He looked at people as alive, not in some silly less than perfect ranking system. Jesus saw people as distinct individuals, alive and beautiful, each in his or her own way. While the religiously right saw many people as irredeemably imperfect and shouted, "Shame! Shame!" he saw potential in each person regardless of his or her imperfections or their past. Jesus called to all the individuals who could hear him during the Sermon on the Mount,

*Each of you is the salt of the earth. If salt has no flavor, can you make it salty again? No. It's purpose is to give flavor to food or else it is thrown out.*

*Each of you is the light of the world. When people get together and build a city, they do not hide it in a valley but put it on a hill so others can come to it. In the same way, why would anyone light a candle or a lamp and put it under a bucket? No, you put it on the table so that it gives light to all the house.*

*So let it be with you. Let your light shine so that others may see the wonder of what you do and give glory*

Jesus' call was not to consider in shame what we are not, but to find our potential and live it out. Each of us is to find our flavor and share it. Each of us is to find our light and shine it. Each of us is to take whatever we have and set it on a hill for all to enjoy!

# Praxis: Becoming a Character

Below are the titles of classic stories. Can you can name the main character(s). The answers are at the end of the chapter if you need them.

*Gone with the Wind*
*Moby Dick*
*Green Eggs and Ham*
*The Scarlet Letter*
*The Call of the Wild*
*A Christmas Carol*

Characters can be thought of as round or flat. Round characters grow, develop, change, and mature each to his or her potential. Flat characters don't grow, develop, change, or mature. They may even resist it. Flat characters aren't boring, they just don't grow, develop, change, or surprise us.

In *To Kill a Mockingbird,* Scout and Atticus are round characters. Jem and Dill are comparatively flat, and most others are really flat. In most Dickens' novels, the secondary characters are all flat while the primary characters are round, especially in *A Christmas Carol.* Ebenezer Scrooge is quite round. He grows, stretches, changes, even surprises us. Scrooge is such a strong character he becomes a type. We say at Christmas, "Don't be a Scrooge." In *One Flew Over the Cuckoo's Nest,* Nurse Ratched doesn't change. She's quite flat while McMurphy surprises continually. In the gospels, the Sadducees and Pharisees are the Nurse Ratcheds of the gospels. They are the flat rule followers who don't grow, question, or change.

As I have studied fiction writers, the most interesting discovery was the power of characters, even on the writers of the stories. For most writers, to my surprise, plot doesn't shape characters, but instead, characters shape plot. Here is what some well-known authors said about the strength of characters,

Stephen King: *I won't try to convince you that I've never plotted any more than I'd try to convince you that I've never told a lie, but I do both as infrequently as possible.*

*I distrust plot for two reasons: first, because our lives are largely plotless, even when you add in all our reasonable precautions and careful planning; and second, because I believe plotting and the spontaneity of real creation aren't compatible. ...*

*My basic belief about the making of stories is that they largely make themselves. The job of the writer is to give them a place to grow.*

George Martin: *My philosophy is that plot advancement is not what the experience of reading fiction is about. If all we care about is advancing the plot, why read novels? We can just read Cliffs Notes.*

Ray Bradbury: *Remember: Plot is no more than footprints left in the snow after your characters have run by on their way to incredible destinations. Plot is observed after the fact rather than before. It cannot precede action... It cannot be mechanical. It can only be dynamic. So, stand*

*aside, forget targets, let the characters, your*
*fingers, body, blood, and heart do.*

Characters drive plot. For many of us, we have a road map in our minds of our life story: what we want to happen, expectations of life, relationships, and of individual people. What can frustrate us to exhaustion is when our life plots don't develop in the way we'd like to write them. We hope that someone, a spouse, a famous or powerful person or corporation, or even God will come along and make sense out of all the senseless drama of our lives. Apparently, neither God nor Stephen King work like that. According to these writers, not only does forcing a plot onto characters make for bad writing, it makes for bad living as well. Only looking backward do any attempts at sense making work. Even in the life of Jesus, prior to Easter, Jesus' life is amazing, yet, still a tragedy and travesty. If Jesus' life doesn't make sense in real time, why should anyone elses?

In this present age, we have become so accustomed to books, movies, and television that we want stories that resolve, plot lines that make clear sense, and stories that have meaning. That's only in Hollywood. Try as we like, we don't get to write our life or create a set to enact our drama. However, We do get to develop our character along the way.

Fidelity to God and the life we're allowed is to live as Christ like as we can, celebrating the potential and possibility in ourselves and others, developing our characters to as terrific a *telos* as we are able, and let the world respond as it will. Perhaps others will recognize the beauty in each of us, if so, wonderful. Perhaps the world will take us out and nail us to a cross. If so, then we're in good company. Many great characters have been lynched along the way. So be it. The great characters can die as easily as anyone can, sometimes even easier. The great characters are not super human. They are, however, but superbly human, each in his or her own beautiful way. They don't form the stories, but stories have a hard time not forming around them, wonders that they are.

Answers to Character Questions
*Gone with the Wind* – Scarlet O'Hara, Rhett Butler.
*Moby Dick* – Ahab, The Whale, Ishmael
*Green Eggs and Ham* – Sam, I am
*The Scarlet Letter* – Hester Prynne
*The Call of the Wild* – Buck
*A Christmas Carol* – Ebenezer Scrooge

## Praxis: Becoming Christ Like

*Christianity does not enter the world as the clergy introduce it, as an admirable art of sweet and mild consolation. Christianity comes as the definitive, the ultimate, the absolute. Christianity comes because God wills it from God's love for humanity. From God's love, God does not allow humanity to alter the nature of God into a nice humane god. Instead, God seeks to transform us into God's likeness.* Soren Kierkegaard

Paul wraps up the Colossians 3 passage on clothing ourselves in love with this admonition, *[17] And whatever you do, in word or deed, do everything in the name of the Lord Jesus...*

As a parishioner and a pastor, I prayed, "...in Jesus name" so many times it had become a thoughtless pattern until one November I called my own actions under question.

We were having our community Thanksgiving Service, the once a year event when all the congregations around ours met together for worship. We were meeting at Congregation Micah, and as was our tradition, we took up an offering for the local food bank. I was praying away, thinking about everything but my prayer, like, "How do they not take up offerings in the Jewish congregation?" "Is this strange to them that we are having an offering now?" (You think the people in the pews are the only ones who don't pay attention in worship?) Deciding it was time to wrap it up, I ended my prayer as I always had, "...in Jesus' name."

I realized immediately what I had done. As a guest leader in a Jewish congregation, I had forced them into praying "...in Jesus' name." Not only were they our hosts for this service, they had also rescued our Vacation Bible School the previous summer by letting us use their facility after we discovered ours to be infested with brown recluse spiders. Their only requirement for our camp's residency was that we eat our lunches outside in case any children brought ham sandwiches. I judged myself as being both quite rude and very nonJesusish during my prayer.

After the service, I apologized to my friend, Rabbi Kanter, "Ken, I'm sorry about the way I ended my prayer. That was very inconsiderate of me."

"We noticed," he said. "But we knew it was you." He gave me grace.

I decided that four decades of praying, "…in Jesus' name" without reflection was long enough. I did a little research, even though "in Jesus' name" is often used as a divine formula for God's blessing, the phrase points less to the power of the name spoken but instead to the identity and responsibility of those who claim the name. In Jesus' day, when you took on the name of someone, it meant you were part of their group, their family. To pray, "in Jesus' name" meant a promise to not only try and pray as Jesus prayed but live as Jesus lived, like any disciple would his teacher. To pray "in Jesus' name" is a pledge to "live continually in Jesus' way."

As Paul encouraged, "Clothing ourselves in love," so, too, does, "In Jesus' name" or "in the name of Jesus" calls us to clothes ourselves as Jesus taking Jesus as our way into the world. Jesus' followers weren't students. They weren't believers. They were disciples - followers seeking to become like the one they followed. The term 'Christian' wasn't a self-proclamation but was applied by outsiders who saw Jesus' followers as Christ-like-ones. The word was descriptive of the lives of Jesus' followers. They acted Christ like, and not by accident. To clothe themselves in Jesus was their goal, to be labeled by others as Christ like, or living in the way of Jesus, was just a sign of their growth toward their goal as they became clear images of their model in every moment of their lives. Church was not a place, not an hour a week, but a way a way into the world living as Christ's contemporaries, living the Kingdom of God into reality. They didn't just pray the Lord's Prayer, they were the Lord's Prayer, and so should we be in our practices and our praxises, our churches, our homes, and our lives, Christ-like ones, all.

# SECTION THREE:
# Moment Practices

*Whether it is the best of times
or the worst of times,
it is the only time we have.*

Art Buchwald

# A Better Question

*The valid test of a student is the ability to ask the right questions. I would suggest that we evolve a new type of examination paper, one in which the answers are given—the questions to be supplied by the student.* Abraham Joshua Heschel

A couple of pastorates past, I was assigned to a community committee consisting of representatives from thirteen different congregations. I replaced another staff member from our church who had attended for two decades. When I arrived, I was asked what congregation I represented. I told them where I was from and whose role I was taking. That seemed to be enough. They didn't need to know any more – not even my name.

I listened and read as word by word we toiled through the bylaws of the organization for two hours. At the end, I raised my hand, told them my name, and asked, "Since I'm new here, can someone tell me what this group does?"

The moderator replied, "That's a very good question. I think we can discuss that next time. I was also thinking that it would be good for us to go from quarterly meetings to monthly meetings. All in favor?" People raised their hands. "Opposed?" No one raised his or her hand. I abstained. How could I vote against something when I had no idea what they did? There was nothing in the bylaws to tell me.

I went for four years. Each month, we talked about what the committee had done a long time ago, talked about the community and what others ought to do, reviewed the minutes from the last meeting, set the time for the next meeting, stressed the importance of coming to the meetings, and then debated how to spend the $2,000 for missions in the budget. Even though we discussed it monthly, we could never reach any agreement by the end of the budget cycle that involved action.

Church can become an activity for discussion and debate over what is and what ought to be with little thought for what is to be done. As I read in a recent book on leadership, "Scholars make poor leaders. They are trained not to decide." The word decision comes from the Latin meaning "to cut off, to sever." Better to discuss things, defer judgment, and refer the matter to a committee for further consideration than to make a decision. Why go on record as believing that the earth is round when someone may discover next year that it's really flat? Wait. Observe. Be patient. There is still time.

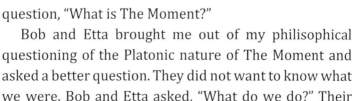

"What am I to do?" and "What does this group do?" used to be essential questions for me. Over time, I lost my better questions until my friends brought me back. When we started meeting together, I was bombarded with the question, "What is The Moment?"

Bob and Etta brought me out of my philisophical questioning of the Platonic nature of The Moment and asked a better question. They did not want to know what we were. Bob and Etta asked, "What do we do?" Their question liberated me from my own mental stuckness. "Ahhhhhhhh," my mind released and my heart opened. "What do we do?" I wanted a label, but they wanted action. I wanted to know, but they wanted to do. When Bob and Etta asked "What do we do?" instead of "What are we?" they offered a different foundational focus.

The world doesn't ache for better answers but better questions and certainly better behavior. One of the challenges of each Moment is to come out of our labeling and defining and focus on our doing. Moments change the primary question for churches and worshipping communities from "Who (or what) are we?" to "What do we do?" making church more than *a building where religious services are held.* Church, like love, hope, and faith, becomes lifeless as a noun, but as a verb, a word of action, church lives. As St. Francis said, "Preach the gospel, and if necessary, use words." We add, "If you must use words, let them be verbs."

The rest of the book is a collection of practices and praxises to help live your moments fully, alone, with God, and with others. Like hymns in a hymnbook, they are not to be practiced all at once privately or in a group. Try them in reflection or worship, in anywhere, at any time, with anyone. Read them in order or skip around. Repeat as necessary. Adapt when needed. Add your own along the way.

## Practice: Say, "For the Moment"

*A king gave one of his servants a challenge, he said, "Go and find a ring that will make a happy person sad and a sad person happy." The servant searched the jewelers and merchants in every surrounding village and kingdom, and then he returned years later.*

*The king asked, "You've found a ring that can make a sad person happy and a happy person sad?"*

*The servant nodded and gave the ring to the king who looked at it closely then said to his servant, "Well done. Surely, this is a ring that can make a sad person happy and a happy person sad."*

*The inscription inside the ring was, "For the moment..."*

To the person with a painful illness or some other terrible burden to bear, "For the moment..." reminds him or her it won't last forever. To the rich, successful, or the young, "For the moment..." can result in grief knowing it won't last forever.

Reminding myself of my moments helps me appreciate them. The poet Shiki pointed out how we can miss our moments with others if we are not attentive,

*When I looked back*
*The man who passed*
*Was lost in the mist.*

64

Shortly after we chose to call our worship time, *The Moment*, I started saying, "...for the moment," and found the simple phrase to be liberating. Here is what the practice looks like for me.

I say, "I'm married for the moment." This is not some ominous expectation of divorce or death, but a recognition that neither Carrie nor I are the same people we were two decades ago. Each of us has changed in ways we didn't expect, plan, or envision. If I don't recognize our ongoing development, then I'll say things like, "You always..." when she actually never alwayses. I will become historical (no, not hysterical). I will bring up prior wrongs, prior slights, prior moments that I never lived in the past but for some unknown reason seem to want to bring them out in the present. There is nothing like the past to ruin the present, nothing like yesterday to ruin a relationship today, and nobody like me to keep trying old patterns hoping for different results. Even though I want to be with Carrie in the moments of our relationship, at times, I seem to come at her. If she does not feel as I do, I try to impose on her whatever emotion I have. When I am "Married for the moment," then I can be with her, sharing a space in time. Yesterdays stay in the past. Tomorrows stay in the future. Now is what we share.

I also remind myself, "I am a parent for the moment." Our oldest daughter just started college. My relationship with her requires a different approach than ten years ago. Those childhood moments are gone. For her to go to college, I have had to grow up, grow into a new phase, and a new way of relating. With all three of our children, when I think I am an expert and know what they need labeling 'their' problems and prescribing for them what they should do, I create distance between us. They are each individuals. What is helpful for one may have the opposite result with another. Being in our moments requires less certainty and more curiosity.

With our new adventure in The Moment, I claimed a new title for myself and use it often as a reminder. "I am Pastor for The Moment." This role won't last forever. How can it? The church is called, "The Moment." Perhaps, The Monument, The Memorial, or even The Movement might offer more longevity. Moments don't last, but they don't have to. Pastors have a great temptation to try and be "meaningful and lasting". Churches love legacies even though lasting is the way of Emperors and Pharaohs. The Jesus Irony is that the one we call 'Savior', in our terms, saves by not saving. He does not try and save the disciples, his family, his synagogue, his Jewish tradition, his nation, his teachings (nowhere does Jesus ever tell someone, 'Write this down! This is really good!" The only time we have a record of Jesus writing anything was in the sand, and we don't know what he wrote. No one saved it.) He does not even try to save himself. He just opens his arms wide on the cross and looks to God in the most horrible of moments.

For adults in our various roles, we are often tempted to try reliving our past to get it right or preliving our future to keep ourselves and those we love free from pain and problems. As a helpful role model to life, Jesus pointed to a child and said, "The kingdom of heaven belongs to people like this child." The Philosopher Heraclitus said similarly, "Time is a game played beautifully by children." What children do naturally that adults don't is let go of one stage of life in order to receive the next. My children, through their years in school, never expected one grade to last. They knew they were there for the year, and at the appropriate time, would leave one grade, one space, one age, for the next. I am trying to relearn from them what I have forgotten as 'Pastor for The Moment.'

I say, "I am alive for the moment." My life won't last forever. I can exercise, diet, avoid poor health habits, but eventually, this life will end. "For the moment..." reminds me of my role while I'm alive - to do my best to live well so that I can die well whenever that moment arises. I am trying to do as my children and learn all I can in each grade, each stage, and then, when my time comes, head into the next.

There is one area I have yet to apply, "...for the moment." I do not say, "My wife is alive for the moment" or, "My children are alive for the moment." I'm just not there yet. As a pastor, I have buried other people's spouses and other parent's children. I am working hard to deny that could ever happen to me. I am certain my acceptance would enrich our time together, but I have some more maturing to do before I give up on denial altogether.

Here is an area that surprises many. I am comfortable saying, "I am David for the moment." In whatever is after this life, will I still be called, "David?" Who knows? Even if "David Whitehill Jones" is one day etched in stone on a tomb or at the base of a statue on the national plaza in Washington like my mother thought, my name may not carry over to whatever is after death. In the Bible, names were changed quite often: Simon became Peter, Saul became Paul, and Sarai became Sarah. If it could happen to them, it may happen to me. For now, "I'm David for the moment."

Try it yourself, say whatever fits, "I'm married for the moment," or "I'm single for the moment." "I'm a parent for the moment,"or "I'm a child for the moment." "I'm a (insert job title, grade in school, or any other roles you play) for the moment." "My name is _____ for the moment." "I'm alive for the moment." And, if you can, "Those I love are alive for the moment."

## Practice: Slow Down

In 1965, a Senate subcommittee predicted the upcoming changes in technology would so revolutionize life in America, and that by 1985, Americans would be working twenty-two hour workweeks and would be able to retire at age thirty-eight. However, the result has been that instead of giving us more time, the new technologies have enabled us to fill every minute of our day as the boundaries of work and home vanished. We can work from anywhere and anytime. Whatever time is left, the list of distractions are infinite.

A more accurate forecast of the future came earlier, in 1955, with Parkinson's *Law of Busyness* (That's busyness not business). The law states,

> *Busyness expands to fill whatever time we have. Busyness is like helium gas released in a room. The gas will expand to fill the whole room, however, as it expands, it becomes less and less dense.*

The more we fill our lives with busyness, the less meaningful our lives and our relationships become. In 1938, Thornton Wilder had little idea of the changes in technology and their effect on life in the next century. What he did know was how the speed of life reduces the quality of life and our appreciation of it.

In *Our Town,* the focal character, Emily, dies while giving birth. She asks the Stage Manager if she can return home to relive just one more day. He reluctantly allows her. She is torn by the beauty of the ordinary moments of each day and her family's lack of awareness of just how beautiful  those moments are. She cries out to her mother,

> *"Mama, just look at me one minute as though you really saw me... just for a moment now we're all together. Mama, just for a moment we're happy. Let's look at one another."*

She stays for a short while and then cries out to the Stage Manager, *"(Life) goes so fast. We don't have time to look at one another. I didn't realize all that was going on and never noticed. Take me back up to my grave. But first, wait! One more look."*

She stares back over her town. *"Goodbye, goodbye, World. Goodbye, Grover's Corners...Mama and Papa. Goodbye, clocks ticking...and Mama's sunflowers. And food and coffee. And new ironed dresses and hot baths... and sleeping and waking up. Oh, Earth, you're too wonderful for anybody to realize you."*

In tears, she looks to the Stage Manager and asks, *"Do any human beings ever realize life while they live it?"*

The Stage Manager sighs and says, *"No. The saints and poets, maybe. They do some."*

Jesus often left his disciples, his work, his family, his friends to go off by himself and pray. He stopped moving and doing to become still and present, focusing on God, and removing all other distractions. In a world moving exponentially faster than the small town of Grover's Corners or Jesus' day Israel, any step away from the speed of life is one of the most important practices.

Poet Gary Gay shows how slowing down and being attentive takes as much discipline and practice as athletics.

> *Weight lifter*
> *slowly lifting*
> *the cup of tea.*

If the weight lifter did everything with the same force, then his tea and cup would likely go flying across the room. The moment of tea requires a different discipline than pushing or pulling a massive weight.

Anytime we go to a community service of worship or spend time on our own in worship, as Jesus did, it takes intention, attention, decision, discipline, and action.

## Practice: Be Here

*When you are measuring life, you are not living it.*
Mitch Albom

In 2011, following the Nashville flood and downturn in the economy, in a time of uncertainty in my life, I prayed to God, "What do you want me to do?"

God responded, "The question is not, 'What do I want you to do?' The question is, 'Who do I want you to be?'" For me, a good sign that God is speaking to me and not just my own voice echoing in my head is when my questions are answered with another question. Apparently, The Socratic Method is not dead with God.

I thought for a minute. Carefully considering my response, then I asked, "Okay, who do you want me to be?"

Silence. No response. No answer. Three months. Six months. Longer, still waiting and left with the question, "Who am I to be?" For a year, I tried being good, competent, successful, effective. I tried being like Jesus, which in my mind, somehow meant being 'nice' to everyone even though few perceived Jesus as 'nice' in the gospels. I even tried being like Old Yellar, yes, the dog from the Disney movie, loyal, faithful, defending his family, sacrificing himself.

I tried being anything and everything I could for about a year. I failed repeatedly at many different things. "Who am I to be?" went unanswered.

After a time of too long silence, God spoke, with another question. "Do you know who I want you to be?"

"Not a clue," I replied.

God said simply, "Here."

"Here?" I asked. I did not understand. In all the things I'd thought to try and be over the previous year, all the roles I thought my congregation and my family needed from me, "Here" never occurred to me. "Here?" I asked again.

"Here," God replied. "You are everywhere but here."

God's challenge to be "here" was not about an address, or a location. "Being here" was about being present in the moments of my life. God's accusation was accurate. I was many places in my mind, seldom was 'here' one of them. I embodied the ancient proverb, "People live their lives like an arrow shot into the air, so busy thinking about where they came from worried about where they might land that they miss all the heavenly glory around them." I was carrying past pain and trying to prevent all future problems. I brought so many expectations to each moment that I clouded my perceptions of people and experiences. I recognized my challenge to be present and the work it would take as Henry David Thoreau encouraged,

*You must live in the present, launch yourself on every wave, find your eternity in each moment. Fools stand on their island of opportunities and look toward another land.*

## Practice: Pray, "Here I am."

Challenged to be mindful of my moments, I found several role models who had been down this path before me. Throughout the scriptures, God speaks to people and the common response is, "Here I am." God calls Abraham who responds, "Here I am." To Moses at the burning bush, God calls him by name and Moses responds, "Here I am." To the little boy Samuel in a dream, God calls, and Samuel responds, "Here I am.

Speak, Lord, your servant is listening," Seeking another servant years later, God cries out, "Whom shall I send," and Isaiah says, "Here am I, send me." The most celebrated response is teenage Mary, responds, "Here am I," and then ends with, "May it be to me as you have said."

"Here" for all those saints and so many others came not on some consecrated mountain or sacred space, but in holy moments, places in time where God and persons met.

When Moses said, "Tell me your name." and God replied, "I AM," God was inviting Moses to encounter God there, in the present moment. What does "I AM" mean if not the presence of God? Certainly for Moses descending the mountain, the holy name, "I AM" was the promise "I AM (Here)." Moses faced Pharaoh ten times aware in each confrontation, "Perhaps this time, Pharaoh will have me killed." How could he have such courage? Each time he went, risking all, but expecting "I AM HERE" to be present.

The contrast between the symbolic pyramids of Pharaoh and God's burning bush is neon. One is a wonder of the world and the other is the work of God. One has outlasted time while the other transcends time. One is built on the backs of slaves while the other is a call to liberate slaves. One puts a governor's power over God the other points to God over governors. One is an attempt to defeat time while the other is a call into moment after moment with God. Finally, one is a an empty tomb and one is a call into life greater than death.

When we end our prayers with "Amen" which means "So be it," they seem final, over, complete. "Amen" feels like we have prayed our prayer and can move on.

Whether alone or in a congregation, ending a prayer with, "Here I am," implies readiness and an openness to God in each moment.

## Practice: Leave Your Nets Behind

To suggest that we might end prayers with, "Here I am" as opposed to, "Amen," is ludicrous. Some might say, "But that's the way we've always done it!" Or ask, "What's wrong with saying, 'Amen?'"

There is nothing wrong with, "Amen." There is nothing terrible about tradition as long as our past patterns don't keep us out of our present moments.

Consider this deep theological question, "Have you ever wondered why the most popular time for Church worship is 11:00?" There is no commandment in scripture where God commands, "Thou shalt worship me at 11:00." The time was set to meet the schedule of dairy farmers so they could milk the cows in the morning, go to church, and then return to the farm for the evening milking. The 11:00 worship schedule is set and followed religiously still in order to meet the scheduling needs of the dairy cow.

According to Alan Watts, "The great symbols of our culture are the rocket and the bulldozer." Each is a conqueror of space. Since we cannot go too much farther in outer space in our era, and there is little land left to explore below the stars and above the oceans, we turn back to time. We try to conquer time by transforming time into another space which we refer to as the calendar and the 'to-do list and fill every minute with as much 'stuff' every day making our schedules as tightly packed as our closets and our attics.

To encounter God, we are called out to a place beyond our understandings of both time and space. Here is my version of an ancient story I heard from Alan Watts,

*Once there was a fisherman. He cast his net into the water. After fishing for a while, he held up his net and looked through the squares and into the horizon. Off in the distance, he saw the mountain. He had been there when he was younger but found the mountain too difficult to climb. Now that he was older, there was something comforting about looking through his net at the mountain in the distance. What he could not climb, he reduced to what he could count and measure The mountain was six spaces across and four high.*

*He took his net with him. Through the spaces, he measured and compared his hut to other huts. That night he had a disagreement with his son, he held up the net to see how many squares tall his son was.*

*Others adopted his way of measuring and made similar grids putting space on parchment and then paper. Even time was transformed to space as days were given formal boundaries on calendars. Moments gave way to minutes and lives transformed to lists.*

*In the midst of this objectifying of time and space walked a rabbi. He approached the shore and some fishermen casting their nets into the sea. "Follow me," he called. They did. He had one initial requirement. They had to leave their nets behind.*

What are your nets? Spaces you use to gain control of your life unaware they can become barriers to the call of God.

## Practice: Attend the Space You're In

*There is not one space and time only,*
*but as many spaces and times as there are subjects.*
Ludwig Binswanger

In high school, perhaps my greatest deception was when attendance was called. The teacher would say my name, "David Jones," and I would reply, "Here," or "Present," and I would be marked as attending. The lie was that though my body was in my desk, my heart, mind, and soul were often elsewhere. Showing up and being marked as present is far different from being present and attending each moment.

One of the greatest temptations in missing a moment is to try to capture it. One of the great ongoing battles at weddings is between pastors and photographers. People want to capture the moment in pictures and miss it. I recently did an outdoor wedding. The photographer was someone I had not worked with before. I made the mistake of assuming I didn't need to tell her not to be a be a distraction during the wedding service. For her, the present was insignificant compared to capturing the moment for prosperity. She danced around, up the aisle, back down, in front of both families, even behind me. It took all my energy to focus on my purpose of guiding the couple through their vows while the photographer was behind me, low to the ground, clicking away. I almost hit her with my Bible. Had I not needed it later, I would have.

Our challenge in special moments like a wedding ceremony, a graduation, or a child's birth is to try and capture the moment for prosperity instead of living each moment as Epictetus encouraged,

*Caretake this moment. Immerse yourself in its particulars. Respond to this person, this challenge, this deed. Quit evasions. Stop giving yourself needless trouble. It is time to really live; to fully inhabit the situation you happen to be in now.*

## Practice: Name Your Nude Karaokes

*Nude Karaoke* was the first sign I saw as I walked up Printers' Alley in Nashville on my way to a bar where Etta and Bob were playing. I was a little stunned by the sign having never imagined such a thing, until then.

"Don't you want to come in?" said a slouched over man on a stool. He was wearing a once white t-shirt that also once fit. "This is a good place for a guy like you," he said. I smiled wondering, 'what did he mean, like me?' He added his next sales pitch pointing to the door in case I was wondering how to go in, "We got nudes." My uncontrollable imagination then gave me a brief image of a bar full of men identical to the man on the stool, naked and singing.

"No, thanks," I said walking onward. A few others spoke to me from different doorways inviting me to come in, but I did not stop and only walked faster remembering my destination.

I am easily distracted. When we moved The Moment worship to a sanctuary in downtown Franklin, Tennessee, the noises from the nearby intersection brought a different set of distractions as we prepared our hearts and minds for worship. The most consistent noise was the automated crossing signals as they beep to let the visually impaired know it's okay to cross. When it is not okay, there is a repetitive, "Wait." "Wait." "Wait." Before our first service, I put up a sign by hammering poles and stakes into the ground. While hammering the first pole into the ground, I heard the voice saying, "Wait." "Wait." I thought it was God and so it took me a half an hour to get the first pole in the ground.

Some distractions come into our lives challenging our inner peace but most distractions we choose. Some nude karaokees may be devilish temptations, or at least shocking distractions, but most are in essence, 'good things'. As Jim Collins describes in *Good to Great*, often it's good that can be the greatest barrier to great. Most life choices are not between good or bad but good and better. C.S. Lewis wrote *The Screwtape Letters* about a senior level demon writing to a lesser demon with advice on temptation. In one letter, he writes about how a simple distraction can tempt us away from significant moments.

*I was once in charge of tempting a fellow who used to go into the British Museum to read. One day as he was sitting and reading, he had a train of thought that concerned me. The Spirit of God was at his elbow in a moment, before my eyes I could see twenty years of work on this fellow tottering on the brink. I had to think fast. I almost lost my head and tried to counter argue with the thoughts the Spirit was putting in his head. But I came up with a better plan. I struck out at the part of the man that was under my control. I invaded his mind with this suggestion, "Isn't it about time to eat? Remember that little deli around the corner? Don't they have a great roast beef? It will be much better to think about this with a fresh mind, after you get something to eat." That was all it took.*

List your distractions noting even the 'good' things which can draw you away from the 'great'.

## Practice: Feel Your Feet

In the Bible, there are some significant moments when feet play an important part. At the burning bush, Moses is told to, "Take off your shoes because you are standing on holy ground." In the gospel of John, on the night of The Last Supper, Jesus washes the disciples' feet. As Moses approaches the presence of God at the burning bush, he must have been aware of his feet, the ground underneath, the heat of the shrub ablaze. As the disciples shared the Passover meal, they must have been conscious of the tingling of their freshly washed feet.

To journey toward stillness, be where you are. Occupy the space you're in. Feel your body from your feet on upward. In the Zen tradition, part of meditation is to give attention to your body, what you're feeling, often starting with your toes and moving to the top of your head, noticing where there is tension and giving it permission to relax. Notice also your holy ground, what's beneath your feet, behind your back, and pay attention to the sounds, vibrations, even smells around you.

## Practice: Close Your Ears to See

*OBSERVE!*
*There are few things as important,*
*as religious, as that.*
Frederick Buechner

To enter your moments, a helpful practice is to close your eyes and listen. Another is to close your ears, or at least ignore your ears, and pay attention to what you see. We become so overly familiar with people and spaces that we know where we are and who we are with so we stop looking.

In Seminary, my counseling professor advised that when we don't understand what's happening between a couple to stop listening and look at them paying attention to where they are sitting relative to others. Who is near and who is distant? Who is rising higher or sinking lower? Jesus was a master at noticing where and how people were from Zacchaeus up a tree to the woman at the well in the middle of the day. Jesus attended where they were and how they moved.

To pray this practice, I use the words of Clara Scott's hymn, *Open My Eyes,*

*Open my eyes that I may see*
*Glimpses of truth Thou hast for me.*

80

*Silently now I wait for Thee*
*Ready, my God, Thy will to see.*

*Open my eyes, illumine me,*
*Spirit divine.*

## Practice: Attend Your Breathing

The most revealing lesson for me in developing our moment practices came when I began to focus on my breathing. I had a lot to learn from this simple process. Breathing shows us how to experience our moments instead of just marking time. While breathing has been something I've done all my life, it wasn't until trying to be present and be still that I attended to my breathing and learned this valuable lesson of the lungs.

Breathing has two simple steps: inhaling and exhaling, receiving and letting go. So basic, so natural, but you can still mess it up. Let me show you. Try this.

Inhale.

Without exhaling, suck in a little more air.

Now, still without exhaling, suck in some more.

Hold it.

Feel like your suffocating?

Notice, you have more air than you can possibly use, yet, you feel like your body is starting to ache from lack of oxygen. Hold the air inside until these words start to look blurry. If you pass out, fall down. When you regain consciousness, from this point forward, don't do everything someone tells you to do, but do pay attention to your breathing.

Breathing is simple, inhale and exhale, receive and release. Life is also simple. It has the same process as breathing, receiving and letting go. As long as we relax, and unless there is an illness or injury to the lungs, breathing will take care of itself, taking in the exact amount the body needs, distributing it through the blood stream, and then releasing so that it can inhale again. Simple.

The part of the process the body does naturally that we seem to find difficult in other areas of life is the exhaling, the releasing, the letting go. We don't like to let go. If we don't release, we can't receive. The body knows just how crucial letting go is, yet, we seldom notice.

Let go to receive what's next.

## Practice: Relax to Breathe

It seldom happened after age twenty, but when younger, from doing a belly flop into a pool or wrestling with a friend, I could have "the breath knocked out of me," when my body got hit so hard it had to reset my breathing.

When working with children who have this experience, I say simply, "Relax. It will come." And in a short period of time, their breathing is restored. It can be scary, for that time which seems longer than the seconds which elapse, it seems that not the breath but life itself is knocked out of you.

Though it seldom happens to me physically, mentally, and spiritually I can have my breath knocked out. I give myself the same message, "Relax. It will come."

In those moments, when you feel that your life has been knocked away, relax, because, like a new breath, new life will come.

## Practice: Release to Receive

*In the hero stories, the call to go on a journey takes the form of a loss, an error, a wound, an unexplainable longing, or a sense of a mission. When any of these happens to us, we are being summoned to make a transition. It will always mean leaving something behind,...The paradox here is that loss is a path to gain.* David Richo

Imagine you are going to swim under water. You take a deep breath and dive downward. After feeling the weightlessness of swimming, your lungs start to ache. Your body needs air. Your muscles may even cramp a little. You stay under as long as you can, forcing your body to do your will. As you head to the surface, you realize you dove deeper than you thought so you reach and pull for the top swimming as fast as you can kicking your legs furiously.

When you reach the surface, what is the first thing you do? Even though you ache to get fresh air in your body, you exhale before you inhale. Finally free from the water, you release whatever is left before you receive. No matter how badly you want air, you must complete the process, letting go of whatever air  remains to make room for your next breath.

Letting go is crucial to receiving and a necessary part of breathing and of life. However, if you breathe as most of us live, even though air is abundant, you will suffocate trying to take in more and more without ever letting go. You will be so afraid there won't be another breath that you'll hold whatever air you have, look for a guarantee for the next breath, take in what you can, only letting go a little, until you pass out or worse. Jesus called his followers to let go in order to receive. (From Matthew 16, Mark 8, Luke 9) "You who want to hold onto your life will lose it. But if you can release your life, you'll keep it," or, in this context, those who want to save air will lose it and those who release it will find it.

## Practice: Let it Go

Moments require the art of breathing. To receive the next moment in life, we have to let go of the previous ones. The lesson of the lungs is to master letting go in our lives in order to receive.

The Britts and I have some friends in Nashville who have inspired us on our journeys. One of our highest esteemed songwriters is Travis Meadows. Here are selections from his song, appropriately entitled, *Let it Go.*

> *I was trouble on legs*
> *like a worn out razor cutting everything I touched*
> *I cut one too many so I figured I'd blaze a trail.*
> *Well I ran like the devil in a house on fire*
> *but I didn't run fast enough*
> *You can run all you want*

*but you can't outrun yourself*

*You let it go*
*What else do you do?*
*You can't hold, what you can't hold on*
*Can't stay young, gotta get old*
*It ain't like you ain't ever been told*
*Don't do no good to complain about*
*the pain you can't outgrow*
*So you let it go.*

Another group we hold in high regard is the McCrary Sisters. They bring with them the power of a freight train as they encourage listeners to, *Let It Go!*

*How can I get rid of this if I don't let it go?*
*I know I can't fix it all by myself.*
*I ask the Lord to help me, over and over again,*
*And before I know it, I take it right back in my*
hands.

*I've got to Let it go! Let it go!...*
*I can't handle it. Let it go!*
*I can't use it. Let it go!*

## Practice: Let Go of Yesterday

*Yesterday is but today's memory*
*and tomorrow is today's dream.*
Kahlil Gibran

Regret is a powerful emotion. Through regret, we try and change the past by reliving it. Nothing ruins the present like bringing the past to the current moment. Through The Moment, we are open to the power of testimony, sharing our stories recognizing whatever was currently isn't, whoever we have been doesn't set who we can become with God's help. Danny Flowers shares his past struggle and present liberation in this powerful song, *I Was a Burden,*

*I was a burden,*
*to my father, my sister and brother.*
*I was on dope, whiskey, and wine.*
*I had given up hope, was losing my mind.*
*I was a burden until the Lord laid his hands on me.*

*I heard him say, "Heal yourself, it's what you must do,*
*forgive yourself, the way I forgive you*
*open your eyes, it'll be alright*
*you can see so much clearer,*
*when you're standing in the light*
*I was a burden until the Lord laid his hands on me.*

*If you are weary, if you are hurting*
*Come on and go with me,*
*one thing for certain, yes!*
*He'll lift you up, set you free.*
*He'll do for you, what He's done for me.*
*I was a burden, until the Lord laid His hands on me.*

Travis Meadows opens this song by giving a short insight to his story. "I moved to (Nashville) trying to be famous. Don't everybody? They got these pictures of me floating around. They got this magazine, *Just Busted.* I made the cover… true story." He shares that in a strange way he was successful in becoming famous as, *The Davidson County Police Know My Name,*

*I came to town to make a difference*
*I had a story to tell*
*I told it loud*
*But my opinion didn't go over so well*
*Waiting for offers, they never came*
*The Davidson county police know my name*

*Now I played in dive bars, forgettable pubs*
*I wrote songs that nobody heard*
*I sold guitars for watered down drugs*
*I rolled all the way to the curb*
*If dumb makes you famous than I can't complain*
*The Davidson county police know my name*

*I'm coming to terms with myself*
*Almost comfortable in my own skin*
*We all stumble on this side of Hell*
*Hell, I might just do it again*
*But I've got no reason*
*To be ashamed*
*The Davidson county police know my name*

*Now I've got more stories*
*I've got more music*
*I've got more songs I can sing*
*I've got more patience*
*And faith now to use it*
*A past and the cracks in between*
*I'm partially broken with parts of me sane*
*The Davidson county police know my name*

*I live for the moments*
*While moments remain*
*I roll with the punches*
*I'm numb to the pain*
*I cry for the prisoners still tied to their chains*
*And the Davidson county police know my name*
*Yeah, the Davidson county police know my name*

Letting go is an art that takes practice. Burying our pasts is required to be born into our present and the new songs in our lives.

## Practice: Receive the Present

When Johnny Few sang at The Moment, he introduced this song by saying, ""I didn't make this one up. King David did. He was a bigger sinner than me." Psalm 5,

*Give ear to thy servant, O' Lord*
*Consider my meditation*
*Harken unto the voice of my cry*
*My King and My God*
*For unto Thee will I pray*
*My voice shall Thou hear in the morning*
*O' Lord, in the morning,*
*will I direct my prayer*
*unto Thee and will look up.*

Johnny shared some of not only his life's story but of how God reaches out to us in these lyrics,

*When I was lost,*
*a sheep without repent*
*He left the ninety-nine*
*and brought me back again.*
*There's no denying,*
*I'm just a pilgrim trying,*
*to follow him.*

In our songs, our stories, our lives, releasing to receive is like the tag line in a gospel song, we can repeat it again and again as needed.

## Practice: Open Yourself Wide

Possibilities, like air, do not require fabrication. Our lives are full of potential once we open ourselves to the possibilities God has for us. Like the many roads before us, we just need to be, as Travis Meadows encourages in this song, *Wide Open,*

*There is a road that'll take you right out of this town,*
*a song that you never want to turn back down,*
*an endless sky running out of ground,*
*wide open.*

*There's gonna be those things you never said before,*
*an Arizona wind on a canyon floor,*
*like the eyes of a child in a candy store,*
*wide open.*

*Breathe, breathe, fill your lungs with better air*
*Reach, reach, like you know it's waiting there*
*I've found, letting go of what you're holding*

*leaves your heart and arms a little more,*
*wide open.*

Pray this practice by asking God for help to open yourself wide to God. Use this prayer by Henri Nouwen to get you started,

> *Dear God,*
>
> *I am so afraid to open my clenched fists!*
> *Who will I be when I have nothing left to hold on to?*
> *Who will I be when I stand*
> *before you with empty hands?*
>
> *Please help me to gradually open my hands*
> *and to discover that I am not what I own,*
> *but what you want to give me.*
> *And what you want to give me*
> *is love, unconditional, everlasting love.*

## Practice: Be Loved

*Until you value yourself, you won't value your time. Until you value your time, you will not do anything with it.* M. Scott Peck

Sometimes, I have John the Baptist living in my head, which can make my brain a very uncomfortable place to be. The Gospel of Matthew describes John like this in Matthew 3:

*4 Now John wore clothing of camel's hair with a leather belt around his waist, and his food was locusts and wild honey.*

If you're going to have someone residing in your brain, I encourage you to choose someone not clothed in camel's hair, it's quite itchy. I also suggest someone who doesn't eat bugs, and someone who doesn't yell. John yells a lot.

*5 Then the people of Jerusalem and all Judea were going out to (John)... 7 when he saw many Pharisees and Sadducees coming for baptism, he said to them, "You brood of vipers! Who warned you to flee from the wrath to come?... 10 Even now the ax is lying at the root of the trees; every tree therefore that does not bear good fruit is cut down and thrown into the fire.*

I heard John the Baptist a lot as a child. For example, I remember when I stole some gum from a grocery store. When my mother found out, she told me she was disappointed in me. What I heard was John's voice "You're a disappointment."

My father didn't have to speak what I could hear on my own. I was the youngest of four children. My older brother was the athlete. It meant a lot for my father for me to play football like my brother. I wasn't quick enough, fast enough, or strong enough. Instead, I was signed up for baseball where it was not the lack of speed, strength, or skill that got me in trouble; it was the lack of attention. Let's see, what was I talking about... Oh, yes, I remember being in the outfield watching a bird flying over the field and the parents on the bleachers. I always wondered where and when a bird would poop and if they just let it fly when they felt like it or aimed it at cars and people. Then I would hear my name called out, "David!" When my name was yelled like that, it meant a ball was coming.

Since attention was a big problem for me in the outfield, the coach repositioned me to first base. Do you know why first base was a guarantee I would focus more on the game? Because in the outfield, the ball might be hit every so often in your general direction, but at first base, several times an inning, a ball was likely thrown at you, about head height. You had to pay attention to survive.

Late in a game, I was going up to bat when my coach said, "David, we can win this one. We really need you to get a hit and get on base." I wanted to please my coach and do what he said, only instead of "We need you to get a hit," I heard, "We need you to get hit." So, I did. I leaned in my left shoulder and the ball hit me high on my back. "Take your base!" the umpire yelled. I took one for the team. I found getting hit was a lot easier to accomplish than getting a hit, after all, my back was larger than any bat. The only problem was, as I got older, the pitches came harder, faster, and were a lot more difficult to keep from hitting my head, so my on base percentage dropped significantly.

Though he never said it, I could tell my father was disappointed that I was not the athlete he wanted me to be. No father sits in the stands and yells, "Come on, Son! Get hit! That's my boy!" With John the Baptist in my head, I heard not that my father was disappointed, I heard, "You're a disappointment."

At school, I found math was like a second language to me. If there were 100 questions, I would get 99 of them right. I was quite the math whiz. The problem was, even though I could get 99 out of 100 questions correct, 9 times out of 10, I would forget to put my name on my paper. The teacher would return our quizzes, paper by paper, and child by child, calling each by name. Then she would say, "This last one doesn't have a name on it." Everyone would look around the room. There was one child left without a paper, me. As she handed me my quiz, she would lean over to me as I was sliding deep in my seat, "I don't know what kind of boy can do so well at math but not put his name on his paper." I knew what kind of boy could. A disappointment. John the Baptist was at it again.

John the Baptist also attended church with me, whether remakes of John Edwards yelling at sinners in the hands of an angry God or John Calvin telling us how our basic nature was total depravity, they all just reinforced John the Baptizer in my head.

I really didn't understand grace or the love of God until March 9th, 1995. That's when our daughter Cayla was born. We named her, Cayla Joy Jones. Cayla means pure and so her name is Pure Joy. As I held my new born daughter in my arms, I loved her simply because she was. I loved her simply because of who I was, her parent, her father. Through a father's eyes, John the Baptist disappeared, and as the heavens parted, I could hear the voice of God.

# Practice: Be *Beloved*

In contrast to the voice of John the Baptist is the voice of God in Matthew 3,

> *13 Then Jesus came from Galilee to John at the Jordan, to be baptized by him. 14 John would have prevented him, saying, "I need to be baptized by you, and do you come to me?" 15 But Jesus answered him, "Let it be so now; for it is proper for us in this way to fulfill all righteousness." Then he consented. 16 And when Jesus had been baptized, just as he came up from the water, suddenly the heavens were opened to him and he saw the Spirit of God descending like a dove and alighting on him. 17 And a voice from heaven said, "This is my Son, the Beloved,[d] with whom I am well pleased."*

This love is from God and rooted in God, not only evident in the voice at Jesus' baptism but when in his ministry the voice comes. Again, this is Matthew chapter 3 with 25 chapters to go. What has Jesus done so far? Nothing. This is the beginning. Jesus has not healed anyone, not walked on water, not confronted wrong doers, not stood up for the poor, not feed 5,000 with 5 loaves and 2 fish or anything else, and certainly not died on the cross or risen again. He has done nothing. Yet, here, God says, "My child. Beloved. With whom I am well pleased." Is God pleased because Jesus showed up? No. God is pleased because God is pleased. Jesus is Beloved because God is beloving. God loves because God loves. This is a different sort of love. It is not about meeting parent, teacher, coach, or the world's expectation, disappointing or otherwise. It is not about setting yourself apart, proving that you are somebody, someone, something special, or even showing the world that you are alive. You are loved simply because God says so. Listen for God's voice and turn away from all the others.

## Practice: Live to Express not Impress

Fresh from his baptism, Jesus is sent by the Spirit of God into the desert to face the devil. What he heard from God at his baptism, his naming, the core of his identity, the love of God, the devil challenges immediately, "So, if you are God's beloved, prove it." Because he was beloved, he told the devil to, "Be gone!"

We often live hoping that God will love us – such a lack of faith! We live not to be loved but as beloved. Etta Britt and Jon Coleman expressed the liberating power of God's love in their song, *You Don't Have to Impress Jesus,*

*You don't have to impress Jesus
with diamonds or a Cadillac car
You don't have to impress Jesus
He loves you just the way you
are*

*No, he don't care what you wear
All that matters is in your heart
Yes to him, is all you gotta say
and its never too late to start*


*So come on down to the river*

*Down to the river and pray.*
*Walk on into the water child*
*And let him wash your sins away*

*You don' have to impress Jesus...No*
*You can't impress Jesus*
*He loves you just the way you are...*

The good news of the gospel is not just that we see the heart of God in Jesus, but that God's heart is full of love for us. With God's love we have nothing to prove but much to express.

## Practice: Pray, "My Father..."

*Have you ever noticed how Jesus healed with no strings attached? He didn't say to blind Bartimaeus, now healed, "Now don't you go ogling beautiful women." To the owner of the withered hand he restored, Jesus didn't warn, "No stealing now."* William Sloane Coffin

When the disciples asked Jesus to teach them to pray, they saw a connection between Jesus' prayer life and his personal life, how he lived. Because they wanted to live like Jesus, they wanted to pray like Jesus. Jesus taught them what we refer to as, "The Lord's Prayer." The first line of the prayer is, "Our Father," in Matthew, or simply, "Father," in Luke. Make it your mantra and pray it repeatedly.

## Practice: Pray, "Abba..."

For some, the image of 'father' or 'mother' is not a positive one as their relationship with parents was full of pain. To declare that God is not an abusive parent, claim a new word. In the following two letters from the early days of Christianity, Paul uses the Greek word for, "Papa," or "Daddy." The word is, *Abba* (Ἀββά).

> Romans 8: *14 For all who are led by the Spirit of God are children of God. 15 For you did not receive a spirit of slavery to fall back into fear, but you have received a spirit of adoption. When we cry, "Abba Father!" 16 it is that very Spirit bearing witness with our spirit that we are children of God,*

> Galatians 4: *6 And because you are children, God has sent the Spirit of his Son into our hearts, crying, "Abba! Father!" 7 So you are no longer a slave but a child, and if a child then also an heir, through God.*

## Practice: Receive God's Touch

*Of God's love we can say two things: it is poured out universally for everyone from the Pope to the loneliest wino on the planet; and secondly, God's love doesn't seek value, it creates value. It is not because we have value that we are loved, but because we are loved that we have value. Our value is a gift, not an achievement.* William Sloane Coffin

As "Music City," Nashville draws musicians from all over the country. There are so many talented musicians in Nashville that when asked if I play the guitar, I always say, "No." Playing a guitar means something different in Nashville than in my home state of South Carolina.

I've been fortunate to watch Bob Britt play the guitar in many venues on many occasions over the years of our friendship. Likely, you've heard Bob play and didn't know it. Sitting in a restaurant, we heard three songs in a row on the radio that Bob had performed with all three bands. When I saw Bob play with John Fogerty at The Ryman, I watched Tom Spaulding, his guitar tech, bring him guitar, after guitar, after guitar. Tom brought so many instruments out for the different songs I commented to Carrie there was nothing left for Tom to bring other than a chair to see if Bob could play it. Tom would later say of Bob in contrast to other premier guitar players, "Bob has a way of seeing the whole and finding his place on stage making room for himself and making the music better at the same time."

Having watched Bob for so many years, from a distance and up close, I finally figured out what amazes me most about him. There are many great guitar players who have created their own particularly distinct and recognizable sounds like B.B. King, Stevie Ray Vaughn, or Eddie Van Halen. Bob does something even more miraculous. At one particular Moment Service, Bob took out his guitar for the night, a *Stella* he had purchased for fifteen dollars at a Good Will. With a slide and pic, he brought out not Bob's sound from the guitar, but the guitar's

sound. The Stella sounded cheap and tinny when I touched it but resonated with life at Bob's touch. In his hands, the Stella reached its full potential. Watching Bob, I remembered this poem by Myra Brooks Welch, *The Touch of the Master's Hand,*

> *Twas battered and scarred and the auctioneer*
> *Thought it scarcely worth his while*
> *To waste much time on the old violin,*
> *But he held it up with a smile.*

> *"What am I bid, good folk?" he cried.*
> *"Who'll start the bidding for me?*
> *A dollar, a dollar ... now two ... only two ...*
> *Two dollars, and who'll make it three?*

> *"Three dollars once, three dollars twice,*
> *Going for three" ... but no!*

*From the room far back a gray-haired man*
*Came forward and picked up the bow.*

*Then wiping the dust from the old violin*
*And tightening up the strings,*
*He played a melody pure and sweet,*
*As sweet as an angel sings.*

*The music ceased, and the auctioneer,*
*With a voice that was quiet and low,*
*Said, "What am I bid for the old violin?"*
*As he held it up with the bow.*

*"A thousand dollars ... and who'll make it two?*
*Two...two thousand, and who'll make it three?*
*Three thousand once and three thousand twice ...*
*Three thousand and gone!" said he.*

*The people cheered, but some exclaimed*
*"We do not quite understand ...*
*What changed it's worth?" and the answer came:*
*'Twas the touch of the master's hand."*

*And many a man with soul out of tune*
*And battered and scarred by sin*
*Is auctioned cheap by the thoughtless crowd*
*Just like the old violin.*

*But the Master comes, and the foolish crowd*
*Never can quite understand*
*The worth of a soul, and the change that is wrought*
*By the touch of the master's hand.*

*O Master! I am the tuneless one*
*Lay, lay Thy hand on me,*
*Transform me now, put a song in my heart*
*Of melody, Lord, to Thee!*

The author of this poem, Myra Brooks Welch, was born into a family of musicians, though she loved music and playing the organ, she was limited by debilitating arthritis and a condition which confined her to a wheelchair. Unable to play music, she put her creative energy into writing poetry. Her friends called her, "The poet with the singing soul." She typed her poetry with two pencils, one grasped in each hand, using the erasers to hit the keys.

Many in Nashville rate a guitarist by the expensive nature of the instrument they play, some with even a model named after them. For those who look close enough, we can see the true masters of the art who can bring life from whatever instrument they touch. So, too, with human life, God is the master who can bring out our potential making us priceless.

When your mind is still, when you are in the present moment free from past valuations or devaluations, be with God, seek out the touch of the master's hand in your life.

Pray this practice opening yourself to the touch of God using Frances Ridley Havergal's hymn, *Take My Life.*

> *Take my life and let it be*
> *consecrated Lord to Thee.*
>
> *Take my moments and my days*
> *let them flow in ceaseless praise.*

*Take myself and I will be*
*ever only all for Thee.*

## Practice: Pray, "Give us this day…"

*The biblical reminder is clear: whatever our economic system, the enemy is excess, not possessions. The battle cry is "Enough!" Not "Nothing." "Enough" so that we can all break bread together, so that everyone's prayer can be answered – "Give us this day our daily bread."* William Sloan Coffin

"The Lord's Prayer" contains many phrases that can lead us into life more in tune with Jesus and his way. "Give us this day, our daily bread," helps us to slow down and enter into each moment. To focus on our daily bread requires an ability to distinguish between what we need and what we want. The current global economy not only encourages no distinction, it is dependent, at least in the short run, on blurring the distinction so wants are treated with the same passion and urgency as needs. And since wants never satisfy when removed from needs, our desires become insatiable. Consider the buying practices and the changes a century has brought.

A hundred years ago, the common practice was:

a. figure out what you need.

b. shop to find out where you can get it and what it costs.

c. figure how you can pay for it.

d. buy it.

Today, there are stores around us and online where we can shop with no idea what we 'need', until of course we see it, then we know for certain. The current process is:

a. shop to figure out what you 'need.'

b. buy it.

c. figure out how you can pay for it. (often because you have to in order to be able to buy anything else)

d. learn what it costs.

The practice of "Give us this day our daily bread" begins by noticing the difference between needs (your daily bread) and wants (your daily banana pudding). Wants feel like needs, and unless we know the difference, we may get everything we want and starve to death or die of loneliness. William Sloane Coffin offers this reminder,

> *There are two ways to be rich: one is to have a lot of money; the other is to have few needs. Let us remember that Jesus – who influenced history more than any other single person, institution, or nation – died, his sole possession a robe.*

Praying, "Give us this day our daily bread," calls us to look beyond those needs we can earn, pay for, and acquire on our own to outside of ourselves, to God. Van Morrison offers a helpful question for reflection on whether or not we are seeking our daily bread from God. Morrison asks,

> *When will I ever learn to live in God?*
> *When will I ever learn?*
> *He gives me everything I need and more*

## Practice: Inhabit Each Moment

*Every day is a journey, and the journey itself is home.*
Basho

Once, when a religious professional wanted to follow Jesus, he asked a simple question but found great disappointment in Jesus' response in Matthew 8,

> *18 Now when Jesus saw great crowds around him, he gave orders to go over to the other side. 19 A scribe then approached and said, "Teacher, I will follow you wherever you go." 20 And Jesus said to him, "Foxes have holes, and birds of the air have nests; but the Son of Man has nowhere to lay his head."*

I feel sympathy for the poor scribe, a dedicated religious professional who was trying to become one of Jesus' disciples; he simply wanted to know where the rabbi was going. His dedication was to go anywhere with Jesus wherever that was. He could not imagine a rabbi without a location, a space, or an address.

Jesus was houseless but not homeless. He was at home in any place, apparently even the cross, though in the tomb he was apparently just passing through.

When Jesus laid siege to Jerusalem, the crowds cried out, "Hosanna!" or "Save us!" Jesus did two surprising things for a king coming to lay claim to a city: instead of coming in on a warhorse, and instead of attacking the soldiers, he went to war with The Temple. When he died on the cross, the veil to the Holy of Holies space within the Temple ripped irreparably, no more allowing the leaders to try to trap God within.

Jesus was never impressed by holy lands, holy buildings, or even holy people, he does, however, seek out holy encounters or holy moments, which can happen anywhere and anytime.

Building a house is a great accomplishment, learning to be at home wherever you are, in every stage of life, in every situation, with everyone you meet is an even greater achievement and far closer to Jesus' way in the world. A great house surrounds you in comfort, but a mature adult finds comfort within and with God. Rabbi Heschel challenged that one of our greatest contemporary difficulties came from not knowing the difference.

*We no longer know how to justify any value except in terms of expediency. Man is willing to define himself as "a seeker after the maximum degree of comfort for the minimum expenditure of energy." He equates value with that which avails. He feels, acts, and thinks as if the sole purpose of the universe were to satisfy his needs.*

Instead of building and protecting a holy building a holy space in a holy land for a place in a holy people, Jesus' way is still to live holy moments, at home everywhere, everywhen, and with everyone.

# Practice: Inhabit Each Moment Heroically

Kierkegaard pointed out that for some, the response to our mortality, our finitude, the sense of our clocks running out is that we can have a sense of despair so intense that it turns us into a terror. Ernest Becker observed something similar. Becker wrote *The Denial of Death* in which he expressed four points:

1. We die.
2. We don't like it.
3. We'll spend much of the time of our lives trying to pretend like we won't die denying death or connecting ourselves to something 'lasting' in our 'immortality projects.'
4. The greatest human evils come from attempts of individuals or nations to be larger than life and deny death.

According to Becker, humans do our worst evils in trying to deny death and make ourselves immortal even if we have to die or destroy others to do it. Consider the classic villains. Are they evil or denying time and willing to do anything to achieve it? In the Bible, Pharaoh built his pyramids to be immortal even if he had to enslave others to do it. Herod had all the babies two years and younger killed when he heard about Jesus' birth from the Magi. His actions weren't personal. He didn't care about Jesus. He was simply protecting his connection to immortality while preserving his place as 'king'.

One of my favorite examples is the iconic vampires. They grasp at life, hoping to live forever even if it means draining the life from others. They become creatures of the dark, afraid of light, afraid of their reflection, living on in time but becoming less and less alive, less and less human, undead, yet, neither dead nor alive.

Following a similar pattern are the following villains: The Wicked Witch of the West from *The Wizard of Oz*; Darth Vader from *Star Wars*; and Valdemort from *Harry Potter*. All these villains, in their pursuit of not dying become less and less alive. The Wicked Witch in Oz becomes more like her flying monkeys. Darth Vader becomes more and more machine and less and less human. Valdemort starts to lose his humanity, in the movies he loses his facial features and becomes noseless. The lifeless existence of these villains exemplify the e.e.cummings quote, "Being not dead is not the same as being alive."

In contrast to the villains, the heroes would give up their lives, but they would not sacrifice their journeys, their growth, or their friends, all which the villains lost long before in their attempts at not dying. The heroes understood there was more to life than not dying, more to love than controlling others, and they became more and more examples of what true heroes are – fully human.

Heroes aren't super human. Heroes are superbly human. They live well, even if living well means dying prematurely. The hero path recognizes there is more to life than not dying. Heroes don't defeat time; they live their moments.

## Practice: Say, "There's no place like now,"

In *The Wizard of Oz*, Dorothy learns that she has the power to find home anytime she wants by clicking her heals together three times and saying each time, "There's no place like home."

To remind yourself to live your moments, to be at home whenever and wherever and with whomever you're with, say three times, "There's no place like now." You can even click your heals together three times if you want.

## Practice: Let it Be

I have difficulty accepting the world around me and letting anything be. I am easily distracted and noise can shatter my focus. My motto is "Let there be peace on earth and let it begin with everyone and everything else." My attempt at gaining peace is by trying to change the world and avoid my inner turmoil altogether. Even though it doesn't work, I keep trying the same thing hoping for different results.

For example, early one morning our house contained sleeping parents and children until a horn woke us up. Apparently, a neighbor was being picked up by his carpool. Instead of going to the door, the driver just sat in the car and blew his horn, again, and again.

I thought to myself, 'I want to be Gandalf (the wizard from Tolkien's *The Lord of the Rings).*' I waved my hands in small circles and hummed. "What are you doing?" Carrie asked me.

"I am magically causing all the tires on their car to go flat," I said.

"Oh," she said.

The horn blew twice next door. I waved my hand again.

"What now?" she asked.

"I'm magically causing their horn to mute," I said.

The horn blew again.

I swayed my whole body from side to side.

"What are you doing now?" Carrie asked.

"I'm causing the car to catch on fire so that the driver will run away, and all will be quiet," I said.

"How's that working for you?" she asked.

I then began waving my hands at her. "Shhhh," I said.

I often catch myself wanting power to control the world, to end all my frustrations by magically and even prayerfully changing current reality to calm my inner rage, yet, with little results.

The *Let it Be* practice is aids our inner peace by letting the world around us be as is.

## Practice: Accept Your Thoughts and Feelings

If our method to personal peace is to try to force peace upon the world around us, we will go unsatisfied. If our practice is to become still souls regardless of the world around us, then what used to annoy us may challenge us. Our energies focus on a different goal. Still minds, hearts, and souls can create potential for deeper relationships than we had thought possible because we had put all our hopes into others changing in order to silence the noise in our minds.

Part of "Letting It Be" involves not just accepting the noise outside of us but the noise inside as well. Besides letting the world be, we can let our thoughts be.

When we sit still and try to empty our minds, usually the opposite occurs. Thoughts and feelings come zooming in. "Letting Them Be" means accepting them without resisting. An even worse barrier to *letting it be* is criticizing yourself for not being able to control your thoughts and emotions.

Accepting our thoughts and feelings allows them to be what they may. Accepting doesn't mean you let them rule you. If you have a thought or feeling during a time when you are practicing being still, let the thought go on its way. If there is a feeling you don't want, acknowledge it, notice it, just don't become it. Like the wind, let it blow by you, and by accepting it, it won't blow you away from the present moment.

## Practice: Say, "Be still," to Stormy Thinking

*Here or there does not matter.*
*We must be still and still moving*
T.S. Eliot

There are times when your thoughts and emotions can possess you, and you do need to respond. Ralph Waldo Emerson wrote, "What lies behind us and what lies before us are tiny matters compared to what lies within us." When anxiety takes over, or when any thoughts or emotions dominate, telling them to "Be still," is a helpful practice. This isn't an act of emotional condemnation telling them, "You're a bad emotion," or telling yourself, "You shouldn't feel that way," but just instructing the turbulence in your mind to, "Be still." It is recognizing that your peace must begin within as Robert Allen described,

*We can only help make our lives and our world more peaceful, when we ourselves feel peace. Peace already exists within each of us, if we only allow ourselves to feel its comfort. Peace of mind begins when we stop thinking about how far we have to go, or how hard the road has been, and just let ourselves feel peace. Peace of mind gives us the strength to keep trying and keep walking along the path that we know is right for our lives.*

A great example of "Be still" in practice is Jesus with the disciples in a storm. The story is found in Matthew 8, Mark 4, and Luke 8. This is Mark's version,

*35 On that day, when evening had come, (Jesus) said to (the disciples), "Let us go across to the other side." 36 And leaving the crowd behind, they took (Jesus) with them in the boat, just as he was. Other boats were with him.*

*37 A great windstorm arose, and the waves beat into the boat, so that the boat was already being swamped. 38 But (Jesus) was in the stern, asleep on the cushion; and they woke him up and said to him, "Teacher, do you not care that we are perishing?"*

*39 He woke up and rebuked the wind, and said to the sea, "Peace! Be still!" Then the wind ceased, and there was a dead calm.*

*40 He said to them, "Why are you afraid? Have you still no faith?"*

*41 And they were filled with great awe and said to one another, "Who then is this, that even the wind and the sea obey him?"*

As a young boy on a boat, trying frantically to get back to shore before a storm surrounded my friends and me, I stood up, held my hands apart, and commanded, "Be still!" Nothing happened. I haven't tried it again. As I've gotten older, I've realized that I often have the same lack of success calming the storms of my mind as I do the storms outside. As I read this passage, I can see the disciples had the same problem. The storm was around them. The disciples were terrified. In their day, they had known many who had gone out in raggedy wooden boats, met a storm, and never returned. Their minds were full of so many intense thoughts and emotions that they were tossed by the waves in their mind.

They woke Jesus who said to the storm, "Be still." Immediately, the storm calmed. Then he asked, "Why are you so afraid, do you still not have any faith?" The word 'still' points to where they have been before the boat ride, what they had done together, what they had seen Jesus do, all that they had experienced. Jesus' question didn't deny the threat of the storm but asked how they could be so unaware that he was present with them. They were not alone.

The story of Jesus' life is framed at the beginning and end by angel bookends. At the beginning, an angel says to a group of shepherds, "Fear not," and at the empty tomb, an angel tells the women, "Don't be afraid." Unless our minds are open, we'll never hear the good news that we don't have to live in fear no matter what the situation. We are not alone.

Say to your stormy thoughts, "Be still," then open your heart to God's messengers, encouraging you, "Do not fear. You are not alone."

# Practice: Accept Your Unchangeables

We often face unchangeable problems. How we face them can keep us from living our moments. We may try to relive the past as if doing so could get it right or prelive the future to solve our problems ahead of time. To come into any moment, especially a moment of worship, it is helpful to recognize where we have power and where we don't as our path to peace can be found in *The Serenity Prayer*,

> *God grant me, the serenity*
> *to accept the things I cannot change,*
> *the courage to change the things I can,*
> *and the wisdom to know the difference.*

To enter into any moment requires not only recognizing what we can change and what we cannot change, but what we can or cannot change in any given moment. If you have a problem which no action is possible right at that time, then the wise choice in that moment is to recognize what you cannot do and be as fully present as possible. Consider Sophia in this crisis as a model for life,

> *Sophia was walking along one day when a tiger started to chase her. Running from the tiger, she hurried along the edge of a cliff and fell over. Part way down, she grabbed a vine stopping her fall.*

*She looked above and saw the tiger looking over the edge at her. She looked below, and there was another tiger at the bottom. The vine she was holding onto started to pull from the side of the cliff. She noticed a strawberry growing on the vine. She pulled it and ate. It tasted very sweet.*

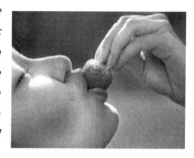

In this ancient story, Sophia hanging in peril can taste and enjoy a strawberry because for that moment, the tiger above, the tiger below, and the breaking vine were all out of her control. She could do nothing to change any of them. What she could do was focus on what she did have the ability to do in that particular moment, enjoy the strawberry.

## Practice: Become Comfortable in Your Discomfort

When we began The Moment, structure, we decided to not use the popular invitation, "If you're looking for a church home, we invite you to come and be a part of our church family here." Church as a 'home' is dangerous. Homes value comfort and convenience. When I go to the local recreation center, I can work out for over an hour, pushing my body to its sweaty limits. However, if I am at home, I will watch the same television station for over an hour because the remote is too far from the couch. When I'm at the gym, the hotter the better. If I'm at home, and the temperature is a couple of degrees off, I complain. When church is a home, we expect comfort, and what we want right when we want it.

My Pastoral Care Professor in Seminary over two decades ago tried to warn me, but I did not listen. He urged our class, "Don't ever use the metaphor of a church family. Families are dysfunctional and choose stability over growth, development, and challenge."

With this church family mindset, seeking comfort and conveinience as our goal, we often promise to those who visit, "Oh, you'll like it here." Especially if they are unhappy at their former church home and looking for a new house of God to call their own, we'll say, "You weren't happy at your old church, you'll be happy here."

For Protestants, the search for satisfying a congregation goes back to the beginning when a furious Martin Luther nailed his 95 frustrations to the door of the church and a new form of church was born. Luther didn't intend to start a new church, denomination, or parish. Luther was actually trying to reform the Catholic Church, but that's what happened. Since then, there is still one Catholic Church with many parishes, but there have been an infinite number of denomination and nondenominational churches and church organizations as protestors leave with the like-minded to start a new church. The Puritans didn't just leave and start a new church, they fostered a new country. As history tells it, "They left to form a new land where they could worship as they chose..." What they wanted was to worship as they liked, with the like-minded. The tradition continues, one after another. To show their unity, they all dressed alike in clear black and white attire.

Like the Roman Empire, the fall of every nation, business, institution, family, and even the lives of individuals begins when comfort and convenience become priorities.

Instead of seeing discomfort as an always avoidable displeasure, a healthier approach is to welcome discomfort as an opportunity for growth, as Scott Peck encouraged,

> *The truth is that our finest moments are most likely to occur when we are feeling deeply uncomfortable, unhappy, or unfulfilled. For it is only in such moments, propelled by our discomfort, that we are likely to step out of our ruts and start searching for different ways or truer answers.*

## Practice: Seek Shalom

*My peace I give to you. I do not give to you as the world gives.*
Jesus, John 14

When I was in seminary, as a pastor in training, I was encouraged to be a "nonanxious presence." This phrase was empty for me. I wanted something more than just being anxiety free. Here is another place the English language is lacking. In English, peace is an absence, *a state when there is no war or fighting.* In Hebrew, peace is a presence. The Hebrew word for peace, *Shalom* (שָׁלוֹם) means *wholeness and harmony.* There is a peace within a person or group (wholeness) and between people and groups of people (harmony). Shalom is so much more than just an outer calm but a peace that is alive and sensed within and between people, groups, and even nations.

Seeking peace can leave us feeling ever empty, seeking Shalom keeps us attending our hunger, our desire for something more than this world can offer, and remaining insatiable until satisfied by a greater peace.

## Practice: Palms Down, Palms Up

One simplified way to think about the differences in churches is what each worship style stresses whether the intellect (Presbyterian), emotions (Pentecostal), or physical movement (Catholic). A healthy balance of all three is an important goal for growth. This prayer method is from the Quaker tradition and involves all three: body, mind, and emotion.

Begin seated with your palms on your knees. Think of something, someone, or some situation you need to turn over to God. Once you envision it, turn your palms upward releasing whatever you need to turn over and opening yourself to God. Trust God knows what you need and continue praying open to God. You may want to verbalize the motions as you turn over your hands saying, "God I give to you my...," or "I let go of..." and then "I ask for..." requesting what you want to receive from God. As an example, "God, I let go of my stress, and I ask for your peace."

You can also combine a breathing practice with this prayer. Exhale as you let go and inhale as you seek to receive from God what you cannot find on your own.

# Practice: Set Down Your Burdens

Into any moment, we can bring baggage, which keeps us from being present. The inevitability of a problem does not mean we have to bring those burdens or challenges in every moment of our lives, especially in times of worship as Sophia illustrated,

> *Sophia was traveling down the road with a bag packed so full the sides seemed about to break open. A man traveling the other way thought this a good time to ask her a philosophical question. "Sophia, why do you spend so much time in prayer?"*
>
> *Sophia slowly lowered her bag to the ground.*
>
> *"I get it," the man said. "When you're praying, you lay down your burden, but what's the point of praying? Does your burden go away? Will your load disappear?"*
>
> *Sophia then picked up her bag and started again on her journey.*

In any moment, we can lay our burdens down. Our time in prayer will then comfort us and give us the strength to pick them back up. Jesus promised rest in Matthew 11, "Come to me all who are tired and carrying heavy loads, and I will give you rest." The rest wasn't a total release from our heavy loads but the rejuvenation to pick them back up again. In Genesis 1 this rest is called Sabbath. It is not an end to all our work, but it is liberation from work in the sacred moments of Sabbath.

The practice of *laying our burdens down* takes recognizing what burdens we carry for ourselves or for others, and being aware when and how we can lay them down. It is not rest that comes automatically on a calendar schedule or something another can give us, but we must claim it for ourselves and receive rest as a comforting and resurrecting gift from God so that we can pick our bags up again renewed for the challenges that face us. *The Book of Common Prayer* contains a prayer with this beginning, "God of all comfort," which sounds like an end to all our problems with God taking our discomfort away. However, *comfort* means *to fortify; to strengthen; to give courage, even power.* The God of all comfort is the one who supplies what we most lack when we most need it so we can continue our journeys.

## Practice: Pack a Pod

Once we become aware of what is bothering us, and can distinguish it from something out of our past or in our potential future, it helps to have an imaginary pod or storage container to put whatever our issues are in it, not matter how temporary. The more stuff you have cluttering your thoughts, the bigger your imaginary container. Some people use an imaginary backpack, but like the attic in our house, I have so much mental stuff, I need a pod.

Counselor and Author Harville Hendrix, founder of *Imago Therapy,* uses a similar technique with couples. In order to make a safe place to hear and be heard, Hendrix let's the couple choose between two roles, the giver or the receiver in an encounter. The one who is going to listen then imagines a container placing all their issues in it preparing to listen and receive what the other has to offer. When the giver feels heard, then the couple switches roles. This practice allows a greater connection between the couple than when each tries to impose their issues on the other.

Using the imaginary pod, rather than build a house for someone, we can do something far greater, make a space for them and for ourselves in relationship. Here are observations from counselors and authors Harville Hendrix and Helen LaKelly Hunt.

> *Most people believe if you're struggling in your marriage you're married to the wrong person. We are convinced that if there is struggle, growth is trying to happen and it's the perfect opportunity for a conscious relationship. At that point, both people need to move beyond the negativity and shift their focus from themselves to the space between. Couples experience a shift when they move from their own need for gratification and embrace the well being of their partner and the whole relationship. At that point a whole psycho-spiritual transformation begins to take place.*

Learn to pack your imaginary pod. Don't try and organize your mental or emotional stuff in it, just cram it in there. When you can learn this practice and share moments with others who can do the same, you'll find safe emotional spaces abound.

## Practice: Own Your Joys, Concerns, etc.

In worship, I often begin formal services with, "Who has joys or concerns?" People often offer things they that they were willing to share publically. In a more personal small group, we begin with, "Who's got stuff?" and we share the more personal parts of our lives. In youth groups, I practice what I learned in camp decades ago in what we call, "Pows and Wows."

In this practice, attend not only what your joys and concerns are, but claim them as your own. If you are concerned about the environment, that concern does not belong to the world; it is your concern, your emotion, something you possess, or something that possesses you. Recognizing where your feelings reside allows you to own them as your own instead of trying to shift the responsibility onto friends, family members, the world, or even God.

## Practice: Feed Your Better Emotions

Often we become our emotions, so full of whatever we are feeling; there is little or no room for anything other than the emotion. We indicate we have become our emotion when we use 'to be' verbs. For example, "I am so angry," or "I am afraid," imply you are your emotions not that there is a larger "you" experiencing them. "I feel angry," allows a recognition of the emotion, and your ability to feel it fully while listening to what your anger, fear, or other emotion is telling you. By becoming aware of your emotions, you can also choose how you will respond as well as learn about your situation from seeing where your emotions are directing you to look. Here is a helpful story attributed to The Cherokee Nation,

> *A boy looked at his grandfather whose face was tight and tense. Seeing his grandfather was troubled, the boy asked, "What's the matter, Grandfather?"*
>
> *He replied, "There is a great war inside me."*
>
> *"A war?" the boy asked.*
>
> *"Yes, between two large wolves. One is dark, stormy, and angry, expecting evil and trying to force me to strike out at others. The other wolf is bright, full of warmth, and light. He expects wonder and joy. He encourages me to give love to others."*
>
> *Now, greatly concerned, the boy asked, "Grandfather, which wolf will win?"*
>
> *The man's face brightened as he looked at his grandson and said, "Whichever one I feed."*

Before the grandfather can decide which wolf to feed, he must see the wolves. To be aware of our emotions allows us to be instructed by them without becoming them and then nurture the ones that are more life enriching. To help you call them by name, create a list of emotions so you will know them when you feel them.

## Practice: Drink Your Cup Fully

Two of Jesus disciples come to him apart from the rest to try to acquire for themselves a position of power in Jesus' inner circle. Jesus uses the image of a cup to illustrate the life he has before him in Mark 10,

*35 James and John, the sons of Zebedee, came forward to him and said to him, "Teacher, we want you to do for us whatever we ask of you."*

*36 And he said to them, "What is it you want me to do for you?"*

*37 And they said to him, "Grant us to sit, one at your right hand and one at your left, in your glory."*

*38 But Jesus said to them, "You do not know what you are asking. Are you able to drink the cup that I drink, or be baptized with the baptism that I am baptized with?"*

*39 They replied, "We are able." Then Jesus said to them, "The cup that I drink you will drink; and with the baptism with which I am baptized, you will be baptized; 40 but to sit at my right hand or at my left is not mine to grant, but it is for those for whom it has been prepared."*

Henri Nouwen takes Jesus' question and turns it into a personal one for his readers to consider,

*Can you drink the cup?*
*Can you empty it to the dregs?*
*Can you taste all the sorrows and joys?*
*Can you live your life to the full whatever it will bring?*

Recognizing the unique particular nature of each moment allows us to receive it for whatever it brings including joy or pain. I frequently sit with families six months to a year after the death of someone they cared about greatly. Remembering Jesus' challenge toward "drinking the cup" that is before us, I point out to them the significance of the person who died. Their pain means the person mattered to them. For example, to a family that has lost a father, if their grief is still strong six months later, we focus on the importance of the person they lost and the painful void they left.

I have often been with adults who have lost a parent and grieve over the lack of emotion they felt. They wanted to hurt more. Even this pain is important as it points to what they missed and to what they want to offer others as adults.

Any loss can be painful. Our challenge is to live each experience fully, Rainer Maria Rilke encouraged,

> *Let everything happen to you,*
> *Beauty and terror*
> *Just keep going*
> *No feeling is final.*

## Practice: Attend Each Particular Moment

Traditions can be dangerous. In families, churches, even nations, a tradition can have us attempting to repeat moments from the past not living each one in the present. Worship, like life, is healthier when it comes out of insight into each moment not just from oversight of an agenda.

When we held The Moment services in sanctuaries, we easily slipped into our personal histories of worship following the traditional patterns without reflection. When we went to different places, we often used the same order for worship, but the specific location and varying congregation awoke us as leaders to each moment challenging us to attend where we were, when we were, and who was with us.

For the four-year anniversary of the 2010 Nashville flood, we gathered at the farm of Carol Warren and Dale Whitehead in Leiper's Fork, a community south of Nashville. We spread out blankets and set up chairs in a field that, four years prior, would have had water over our heads. Attending to the particular moment of worship, with families and individuals who had either been flooded or helped others, Bob Clement shared, *The Rain,*

*It keeps me quiet inside don't you know*
*But it's tearing up my mind inside out*
*To know that I'm bound to live through at least one more day*
*Waiting for the rain to stop it's falling down*

*But I can take the rain*
*And I can take these clouds*
*I can stand this wind that's whipping through me now*
*I been taught to hold on*
*Till the rain has stopped it's falling down*

*It can slow my soul right down to nearly nothin'*
*Just starring at nearly nothing through a window pane*
*But I know every drop that falls*
*Is gonna leave just a lil bit closer*
*To when the rain has stopped it's falling down*

# Practice: Welcome Silence

Floods are reality as well as symbolic of overwhelming experiences in life which challenge our endurance. The poet Basho framed the challenges of floods in this image,

*In the season's rain
the crane's long legs
have      suddenly      been
shortened*

The crane has adequate ability to stand in the river, but when the water rises, even the crane finds his ability taxed to the limit.

Following the Nashville flood and the flooding of their farm and home, Carol Warren and Dale Whitehead wanted to express their experience in a song (as songwriters often do). The problem was, as with most trauma, they had no words, so they wrote, *Words Won't Come,*

*The landscape changed while I was away
Found it just re-arranged, nothing more to say
Barn in the trees, the water left it there
Things that it held- like other memories-
scattered anywhere...*

*And words won't come
Words won't come*

*Breathe in the bottom land, and then ask me why*
*Stir up the sand, unpredictable skies*
*Dig in the dirt, then carry the tune*
*We've known hurt, but always knew what to do....*

*Now words won't come,*
*Words won't come*

*Now I'm mapping the route, and washing the blood*
*Drank through the drought, and swept out the flood*
*Lost half the crop and most of my mind*
*No pen to paper can save me this time*

*Cause words won't come*
*Words won't come*

## Practice: Expect God in the Shadows

Psalm 23 offers a significant linguistic change that is often unnoticed. See if you notice the change in the way the writer speaks of God in the Psalm here in the familiar King James Version,

*¹The LORD is my shepherd; I shall not want.*
*²He maketh me to lie down in green pastures:*
*he leadeth me beside the still waters.*
*³He restoreth my soul:*
*he leadeth me in the paths of righteousness*
*for his name's sake.*
*⁴Yea, though I walk through the valley*
*of the shadow of death,*
*I will fear no evil: for thou art with me;*
*thy rod and thy staff they comfort me.*

*5Thou preparest a table before me*
*in the presence of mine enemies:*
*thou anointest my head with oil;*
*my cup runneth over*
*6Surely goodness and mercy shall follow me*
*all the days of my life:*
*and I will dwell in the house of the LORD for ever.*

In the beginning of the Psalm, the writer speaks of God in the third person, "The Lord is my shepherd...," "He maketh me...," "He leadeth me...," but in the "valley of the shadow of death," the Psalmist changes tenses to the more personal second person. God is "You," or in The King James, "Thou."

*I will fear no evil, for Thou art with me.*

Pray this practice by praying this line multiple times reminding yourself that God is ever present in all the moments of your life, but especially in the shadow times.

Pray this practice by putting personal words to God rewriting the whole Psalm. Here is my version as an example.

*Lord, You are my shepherd.*
*You guide me down the right path,*
*to green pastures, by quiet waters,*
*where You restore my soul.*

*I trust and am not afraid,*
*even in the darkest valley*
*where death seems all around*
*I trust and am not afraid*

*because You comfort me.*

*You prepare me a table,*
*You anoint my head,*
*You fill my cup.*
*I trust and am not afraid,*
*because in Your house*
*I will dwell forever.*
*Lord, You are my shepherd.*

## Practice: Pray, "You Are the Way for Me,"

There are other prayers which can help you look for God in your dark times. During World War II, while in a German prison awaiting execution, Dietrich Bonhoeffer prayed this prayer,

*In me there is darkness,*
*but with You there is light.*

*I am lonely, but You do not leave me.*
*I am feeble, but You give me help.*
*I am restless, but You give me peace.*
*In me there is bitterness,*
    *but with You there is patience.*

*I do not understand Your ways.*
*but You are the way for me.*

*Restore me to liberty,*
*enable me to live free, now,*
*that I may answer before You,*
*and before me,*

*whatever this day may bring.*
*Your name be praised.*

Pray this practice by using this prayer or adding just the phrase, "I do not understand Your ways, but You are the way for me."

## Practice: Count Your Potential Blessings

Three days before the beginning of May, 2010, I got a haircut. I got it cut short because, at that time, I was planning on going to Mexico with my men's group. We were going to build a shanty for a family who didn't have a house. After my trim, my stylist said to me as I was leaving, "Have a blest day," and added as I was walking out the door, "Have a blest weekend and a blest week."

Before my blessed weekend was over, our church, homes of my friends, and many homes and businesses around Nashville had flooded. We canceled our men's mission trip as we became a mission. I blame it on the guy who cut my hair blessing me as I was leaving.

As the buckle of the Bible Belt, for many around Nashville, "Have a blessed day," has replaced, "Have a nice day." I don't believe that those who wish such things have considered what Jesus considers as blessings from God. If so, why would anyone wish such things on another, especially on someone who just came in for a haircut?

Consider Jesus' Beatitudes, or "Blessings" in Luke 6,

*Then Jesus looked up at his disciples and said: "Blessed are you who are poor, for yours is the kingdom of God.*

Shortage as a blessing is far from our American dreams. Our heroes are those who go from poverty to riches not someone who loses riches and becomes poor. We want the Kingdom of God while enjoying our wealth and living in our comfortable personal kingdoms at the same time. Here are other outlandish blessings of Jesus.

*Blessed are you who are hungry now, for you will be filled.*
*Blessed are you who weep now, for you will laugh.*
*Blessed are you when people hate you, and when they exclude you, revile you...*

When someone tells me to "Have a blessed day," I just hope God is not listening. I want the popular definition of "blessings," not the biblical one. I want God to 'bless' me with wealth, health, and happiness. However, faith is trusting that God can take any and all of our experiences and bring something wonderful. Why else would we call the day Jesus was crucified, "Good Friday" if not a profession that with God, any experience could be not only blessed but a blessing?

Facing potential death, Adam and Eve in Genesis 2 ran from God, forgot their relationships, and focused on an object, an apple. They talked about God but not to God. Focusing on an object, the apple, the tried to objectify God. Then they tried to be safe by running and hiding, camouflaging themselves in leaves seeking security by blending into the world around them. God had to seek them out, "Where are you?" "Why are you hiding?" "What are you doing?"

When faced with his death, Jesus did not focus on an object, did not run from God or others, did not hide, did not blend in, faced others, spoke to them, and did not speak about God but repeatedly to God, crying out, "My God! Why have you left me alone?" In contrast to Eden, Jesus seeks God, "Where are you?" "What are you doing?" "Why are you not with me?" Even on the cross, though abandoned by family, friends, and followers, Jesus looked for God trusting that God had not abandoned him though all seemed otherwise. Jesus trusted that even the worst torture the world could imagine might be a blessing for himself and for others in the hands of God. He trusted that even death could be a doorway to new life.

In this life, caught in the temporary, if we want the blessing of wealth, then we should find a high paying career. If we want the blessing of health, we should find a good doctor, dietician, and personal trainer. If we want the blessing of appreciation and validation for our talents, we should get a fan club. But if we want to find the blessing of strength in our weakness, success in our failures, wholeness in our brokenness, and life in our deaths, then we can only get those blessings from God. Why look to God for things we can find somewhere else? Instead, look to God for blessings greater than the world can give and greater than we can claim on our own.

The life of faith is to approach every situation and experience as a potential blessing, no matter what it is, when in God's hands. Like Jesus, the faithful are called to treat objects for what they are, just things, to speak to others rather than about others, to speak to God more than about God, and to seek God in every moment trusting that all can work for good in God's hands, as Paul encouraged in Romans 8,

> *All things can be used for good in God's way. If God is for us, what does it matter who is against us?*
>
> *Can anyone separate us from the love of Christ? Can hardship, distress, persecution, poverty, famine, or violence? Even if we are killed all day long? Slaughtered like sheep?*
>
> *No! In everything, we are far more than conquerors through the One who loves us. I am confident that neither death nor life, angels nor rulers, things present nor things to come, nothing high or low or anything else in God's creation can divide us from the love of God we see in Christ Jesus our only Master.*

## Practice: Attend Your Crossroads

Martin Guitars had an ad campaign called, "Crossroads." In the ad, they retell the legend of Robert Johnson's encounter with the devil.

> *It's a gloomy night at a crossroads on a rural Mississippi plantation in the early 1930's. A struggling blues musician named Robert Johnson has a burning desire to play his guitar better than anyone else. At this lonely intersection, the Devil waits for Johnson. With the moon shining down, the Devil plays a few songs on Johnson's guitar. When Robert Johnson gets his guitar back, he has complete mastery over the instrument. His soul*

*now belongs to the supernatural being, and for the next 5 years or so, he creates music that will live past his tragic, suspicious death in 1938 at the age of 27.*

A closer look at the lyrics of *Crossroads* shows not a man struggling with the devil and fame but with loneliness and pain. The crossroad is whether or not his pain will overwhelm him or whether or not he can come through it with a song. Here are  selections from Robert Johnson's *Crossroads*,

*I went to the crossroad fell down on my knees*
*Asked the Lord above "Have mercy, now*
*save poor Bob, if you please*

*Standin' at the crossroad*
*I tried to flag a ride*
*Didn't nobody seem to know me*
*everybody pass me by*

*You can run, you can run*
*tell my friend-boy Willie Brown*
*Lord, that I'm standin' at the crossroad,*
*I believe I'm sinkin' down*

The song points to a different challenge of life than the struggle with Satan. The trial is to take the pain of life and turn it into a song. As Richard Rohr put it, "Pain that you can't transform, you'll transmit." The great creative power of humanity is to take pain and turn it into art. That was Robert Johnson's challenge, though he did not endure his pain for very long, he furthered The Blues, a music style founded upon turning tragedy into music. Pain transformed to song is the basis of not only the blues but of faith. The Bible's song book is full of similar songs of lament, of struggling between what we long for and what we have, where we are and where we hope to be, and songs like Robert Johnson at the crossroads, that are looking not for the devil, but for God like in Psalm 13,

> *1 How long, O Lord? Will you forget me forever?*
> *How long will you hide your face from me?*
> *2 How long must I bear pain[a] in my soul,*
> *and have sorrow in my heart all day long?*

## Practice: Visit Despair, but Don't Live There

Soren Kierkegaard wrote of the blues calling it, "Despair," and "the sickness unto death." Despair can kill, but to never feel it, to not have experienced heart-wrenching pain is to not be alive. According to Kierkegaard, in our development from infancy to childhood and beyond, we begin to become aware of our existence, to notice that we are here. This awareness stirs in us a sense of awe, wonder, and amazement. During infancy, we become aware that we can intentionally move our fingers, toes, and cry and someone will come. We are alive and become aware of it. We are here and become aware that we are here.

Subtly, over time, we become aware of the limits of our being here, a toy breaks, a pet dies, perhaps we get sick, a friend or grandparent dies. Kierkegaard points out that this is the second part of our awareness, a second stage, where we become not only aware that we are here, we also start to realize that we will not always be here, aware that all which lives, dies.

Initially, there is denial. The temptation is to be special, to be spectacular, other than human. The devil tempted Jesus to try and be special, turn a stone to bread, throw yourself from the top of The Temple in the center of town for all to see, or take control of the world and fix it, be special, be significant, be something other than human, a superior human, better than others, other than mortal. Our existence, when fully attended, takes us to a place where we recognize the limits of life and the undeniable nature of death and can look beyond ourselves to the immortal. According to Kierkegaard, "(Despair) is the road we all have to take – over the Bridge of Sighs into eternity."

If we want God to remove our challenges, to help us deny our weakness, our mortality, we will find God greatly disappointing as Robert Farrar Capon wrote that Jesus is like a lifeguard who sees a drowning girl. He swims out to her, drowns with her, then three days later comes out of the sea promising that everything, even the girl who drowned, is wonderful.

We want a lifeguard who always saves us, who prolongs our life, not one who helps us die to find new life. God is not a life preserver but a life giver. Our greatest problem with God is God's contentment with our mortality, a reality that drives us to despair.

According to Kierkegaard, experiencing despair is not a sin, living there is. Kierkegaard wrote,

*Whether you are man or woman, rich or poor, dependent or free, happy or unhappy; whether you bore in your elevation the splendour of the crown or in humble obscurity only the toil and heat of the day; whether your name will be remembered for as long as the world lasts, and so will have been remembered as long as it lasted, or you are without a name and run namelessly with the numberless multitude; whether the glory that surrounded you surpassed all human description, or the severest and most ignominious human judgment was passed on you -- eternity asks you and every one of these millions of millions, just one thing: whether you have lived in despair or not, whether so in despair that you did not know that you were in despair, or in such a way that you bore this sickness concealed deep inside you as your gnawing secret, under your heart like the fruit of a sinful love, or in such a way that, a terror to others, you raged in despair. If then, if you have lived in despair, then whatever else you won or lost, for you everything is lost, eternity does not acknowledge you, it never knew you, or, still more dreadful, it knows you as you are known, it manacles you to yourself in despair!*

To live fully requires facing death, moving through our frailty with God's strength. We fear death; God mocks it. We live trying to be everlasting in life without death, God offers us life beyond comprehension and understanding. We try to achieve immortality while God gives it freely through our mortality. We want to be free from dying while God wants to liberate us from the fear of dying. We have no power to give ourselves life beyond death any more than we gave ourselves life at birth. Birth was not an achievement but a process, so, too is death into life. Like birth, life in death comes as a gift from God. We do the dying; God does the resurrecting, not just in our final deaths, but our momentary ones, as we let go and look to God for the gift of the next moment, and the next, and the...

## Practice: Turn Your Blues into a Song

Sometimes the blues can come when we get exactly what we've been working for, like our children growing up. Bob and Etta love their daughters, Hannah and Bonnie. They have loved each on their journey from birth to adulthood. Etta faced her blues and turned them into a song in, *Quiet House,*

> *I don't know why I'm up this early.*
> *I guess I'll just make some coffee.*
> *Stare out the windows*
> *and read another magazine.*
> *Try to keep myself busy.*
>
> *In my mind I hear their voices.*
> *The pitter patter of little feet.*
> *Laughing and fighting*
> *and crying as they run to me.*
> *I don't know why I'm up this early.*

*All alone in a quiet house.*
*With far too many things*
*for me to think about.*
*The silence is deafening*
*and the pain of remembering*
*All the beautiful memories of my life.*

Etta reminds me of what I dislike about The Blues in general, the songs are just so damn sad. Only the brave can look at the pain in life and call it "beautiful" as she does here, "The silence is deafening, and the pain of remembering, all the beautiful memories of my life."

## Practice: See the Benefit of Your Blues

Gary Nicholson has written some of my favorite songs. He wrote, *Use the Blues* with this challenge, "Somebody singing about the trouble they had will make you feel better about feeling bad. You've got to use the blues to make you feel better."

In *Shadow of a Doubt*, Gary writes a modern day Psalm, helpful in the blues and out. Notice the bold leap of faith, as he does not ask God to take his struggle away or even make it easy, but to help him keep working until he can work it all out.

*Just another homesick child*
*Tired of running wild*
*Ready to stand trial and move on*
*Though I'm guilty in your sight*
*Have some mercy tonight*
*I can't make it through the fight alone*

*Oh but lord, no don't make it easy*
*Keep me working till I work it on out*
*Just please shine enough light on me*
*Til I'm free from this shadow of doubt*
*Keep me out of the Shadow of Doubt*

*As I try to make some sense*
*Of this world I'm up against*
*Well I know my best defense is your love*
*When the struggle gets insane*
*And the lesson's full of pain*
*Keep me calling out your name with Love*

## Practice: Attend Your Need for Others

*Help! I need somebody!*
The Beatles

Often in religious communities, we adopt a persona of health, ease, and control, denying all needs, including our need for others. If we are honest, then only with help from others can we ever live life beyond our struggles and find pathways out of our personal experiences of powerlessness and despair. With stark honesty, Danny Flowers offers, *Reason to Try*,

*I washed my hands.*
*at the end of the day.*
*all my troubles down the drain.*
*You give me shelter*
*where I can lay my head*
*to ease my burden of pain.*

140

*Man I work for,*
*he tries to steal my dreams*
*sometimes all I can do is cry.*
*Life is so hard,*
*sometimes I want to lay down and die,*
*but you give me reason to try.*

*Bills are outrageous,*
*my health is a mess*
*insurance won't cover the pain.*
*You still love me*
*Stay right by my side*
*No matter what trials the world may bring.*

*You know I'm out doing,*
*the very best that I can,*
*and you never ask me why.*
*My life is so hard,*
*sometimes I want to lay down and die,*
*but you give me reason to try...*

We look to others not only when we have struggles in our own lives and when God seems distant, like this song from Travis Meadows, *God Speaks to Me Through You,*

*Seems like every time I turn around*
*I'm reaching out for answers I can't find*
*Just when I think I don't need help*
*There's two more steps I don't have strength to climb*
*My prayers just hit the ceiling*
*Fall down so heavy I can feel them*

*You can change my world*
*Can change my mind*
*With just one word when you believe it*
*Me, I don't know much*
*But I know love*
*And that's enough to one who needs it*
*When God ain't getting through*
*God speaks to me through you*

## Practice: Expect God's Help in Tough Times

Many of the best storytellers I've heard come from the state of Mississippi. Like Jerry Clower put to music, Paul Thorn is not just a joy to listen to but is an experience in concert or in person. He shares some of his life's story including his career as a professional boxer in, *I'd Rather Be a Hammer Than a Nail,*

*My bossman said you'd better get to work*
*before I have to let you go*
*He just walks around and he pays no mind*
*to the sweat drippin' off of my nose*
*but after twelve long years of him doggin' me*
*out*
*there's one thing I've learned well*
*I'd rather be a hammer than a nail*

*If you've ever been on the receiving end*
*then you'd know what it's like*
*a losin' situation has been the story of my life*
*but I ain't gonna let it beat me down*
*and someday I'll prevail*

*I'd rather be a hammer than a nail*

*I climbed in the ring with Roberto Duran*
*and the punches began to rain down*
*he hit me with a dozen hard upper cuts*
*and my corner threw in the towel*
*I asked him why he had to knock me out*
*and he summed it up real well*
*he said, "I'd rather be a hammer than a nail*

Paul shares more of his background including his wide range of role models when he was a child and what he learned from them in, *Pimps and Preachers,*

*My daddy had a Cadillac, my uncle drove a Ford*
*One was Satan's Angel, and one worked for the Lord*

*One drug me through the darkness*
*One led me to the light*
*One showed me how to love*
*One taught me how to fight*
*I guess you can say I am an overachiever*
*And I owe a debt of gratitude to pimps and preachers*

*Stand there and do nothing but if you want to go far*
*Don't try to please everybody and be proud of who*
*you are*
*Get out there in the game, don't sit up in the bleachers*
*That is the philosophy of Pimps and Preachers*

As one final example, Paul shares about his relationship with God, or perhaps better said, God's relationship with him. He gives, "The Lord is my shepherd," a new image in *800 Pound Jesus,*

*I saw a garage sale, pulled up in the yard*
*Found a statue of Jesus that was eight feet tall*
*He held out his arms, and he seemed all alone*
*So I loaded him up, and I drove him home*

*Out by my driveway he looks down the street*
*long hair and sandals made of rebar and concrete*
*I painted him white with a long purple robe*
*He's the rock of ages on a gravel road*

*He's an eight-hundred pound Jesus*
*Standing taller than a tree*
*He's an eight-hundred pound Jesus*
*A bigger man than you or me*

*I thought losing my job was the end of the world*
*Til my best pal ran off with my best girl*
*I felt suicidal with no real friends*
*So I walked outside with a rope in my hand*

*Out by that statue there's a big oak tree*
*So I stood on his shoulders, and I counted to three*
*I had every intention of buying the farm*
*But when I jumped off he caught me in his arms*

*I wanted to return the favor to him*
*Cause I never had a more solid friend*
*So I planted some flowers, all around his feet*

*And I bought him a flock of ceramic sheep*

## Practice: Sing Songs of Comjoyment

Only a limited singer can sing in a single key or songs of a sole genre. Turning our blues into song is wonderful. So is turning our joy into songs.

Sigmund Freud thought human life was spent seeking pleasure and avoiding pain. The path of the healthy, the fully alive, is to live seeking something more than avoiding pain and trying to find pleasure, Author Sam Keen encouraged seeking something which far surpasses pleasure – passion! He wrote,

> *In the degree that I cease to pursue my deepest passions, I will gradually be controlled by my deepest fears. When Passion no longer waters and nurtures the psyche, fears spring up like weeds on the depleted soil of abandoned fields. I suspect that the major cause of the mood of depression and despair and the appetite for violence in modern life is the result of the masses of people who are enslaved by an economic order that rewards them for laboring at jobs that do not engage their passion for creativity and meaning.*
>
> *I think we need a new word –* comjoyment *– as a companion to* compassion*, to remind us that our greatest gift to the world may be in sharing what gives us the greatest joy.*

## Practice: See Others – *Sowu Bonah*

Technology has added distance to our relationships. Instead of having to find someone and speak to them in person, body to body, voice to ear, we have a computer, phone, or tablet to be a mechanical buffer. Human interaction in which people are actually present and attentive to one another is becoming increasingly rare. Poet Mykal Board captured the distance in human relationship with this poem:

*through binoculars*
 *a woman looking at*
 *me*
*through binoculars*

Bill Moyers critique of our addiction to our technology, machines and all things mechanical in our society is this, "Our children are being raised by appliances."

Rather than text someone, see someone, be present, share the moment. In a real connection, something greater exists as each calls the other into being.

In South Africa is a greeting, "Sowu Bonah" which literally means, "I see you." It is one of the most common greetings of the tribes of Northern Natal in South Africa. It is as common as "hello" is in English. "Sowu Bonah," I see you, might be responded to by another member of the tribe with, "Si Conah", I am here. The order of the exchange is important because until you see me, I do not exist. When you see me, you bring me into existence.

Taking time to see and be seen is a good practice to substitute for our interaction with machines, not the other way around.

# Practice: See Others Through God's Eyes

Jesus connected loving ourselves and loving others as inseparable. The two great commandments are, "To love God with all your being (in every moment), and to love others as you love yourself." We can't love others if we despise ourselves nor can we love ourselves if we need to berate or belittle them to feel valuable or loved. To love ourselves is to see ourselves and others through God's eyes as Martin Luther King taught,

> In the final analysis, says the Christian ethic, every man must be respected because God loves him. The worth of an individual does not lie in the measure of his intellect, his racial origin, or his social position. Human worth lies in relatedness to God. An individual has value because he has value to God. Whenever this is recognized, "whiteness" and "blackness" pass away as determinants in a relationship and "son" and "brother"("daughter" and "sister") are substituted.

Not only is the love of others connected to our love of self, so is the love of others connected to God. The writer of 1 John points out what should be obvious in 1 John 4,

> *18* There is no fear in love, but perfect love casts out fear; for fear has to do with punishment, and whoever fears has not reached perfection in love. *19* We love because he first loved us. *20* Those who say, "I love God," and hate their brothers or sisters, are liars; for those who do not love a brother or sister whom they have seen, cannot

*love God whom they have not seen.[21] The commandment we have from him is this: those who love God must love their brothers and sisters also.*

## Practice: Attend Your Need for God

*Because God has made us for Himself,
our hearts are restless until they rest in Him.*
St. Augustine of Hippo

The first book our men's study group read together was by A.W. Tozer. What impressed us most about the book wasn't the writing, but how he wrote it. Tozer wrote on his knees as an act of devotion to God. Such posturing before God put us in awe. Tozer described our lives well when he wrote this fifty years ago,

*Modern civilization is so complex as to make the devotional life all but impossible. It wears us out by multiplying distractions and beats us down by destroying our solitude, where otherwise we might drink and renew our strength before going out to face the world again.*

Paul warns against speeding through life to the point of exhaustion and missing the important moments as he advises in Romans 13,

*Make sure that you don't get so absorbed and exhausted in taking care of all your day-by-day obligations that you lose track of the time and doze off, oblivious to God. The night is about over, dawn*

*is about to break. Be up and awake to what God is doing!* (The Message)

Paying attention to our breath, living our moments and moving from one to the next, reminds us that what we seek in this life is far more than this life. In our moments, we touch the eternal, and we encounter God who is beyond time itself. The perceived great enemy, time, in contrast to God is not that great after all.

In the Bible, 'breath' points to God and the need for God. In Genesis 2, God forms a person out of mud, breathes into the person's nostrils the air of life, and the person becomes alive. In Ezekiel 37, God sends wind from every direction and blows breath back into some dead bones, and they live. In Matthew 5, Jesus says, "Blessed are those who are poor in Spirit, for theirs is the Kingdom of God." In the language Jesus spoke, the likely word here was not *spirit* but *breath*. A closer version of what Jesus said was, "Blessed are you when you are poor in the breath of God, for you will find the kingdom of God all around you."

If we do not recognize our need for God, we will try to fill the void in our lives with tangible objects or trivial pursuits. When we recognize our need for God, then it will become as Paul Tillich described, "Our ultimate concern," or as an unknown sage encouraged long ago, "Look for God as a person with his head on fire would look for water."

Pray this practice through the words from Edwin Hatch's hymn, *Breathe on Me Breath of God,*

> *Breathe on me, Breath of God,*
> *fill me with life anew,*

149

*that I may love what thou dost love,*
*and do what thou wouldst do.*

*Breathe on me, Breath of God,*
*till I am wholly thine,*
*till all this earthly part of me*
*glows with thy fire divine.*

## Practice: Meet God in Your Moments

The other night, I had a nightmare. I dreamed of Moses, called by God at the burning bush, descending the mountain to go and liberate the Israelites from slavery. But instead of guiding God's people out to meet God into the desert for holy moments, he and the Israelites stayed in Egypt. Instead of living out his calling, Moses wanted to be a consensus builder. Instead of confronting Pharaoh, Moses negotiated a deal with the Egyptian taskmasters where the slaves would stay in Egypt, building pyramids and other wonders of the world. As part of the negotiation, Pharaoh would give the Israelites straw for the bricks to make their labor easier. Pharaoh would also allow them to take the Sabbath off to rest and worship. Pharaoh even allowed them to become 'citizens' though they still had to work like slaves.

Pleased with the peace he had brought to the land, Moses took a position on Pharaoh's Cabinet as the head of The Department of Labor. To make sure the will of God was being accomplished, Moses checked regularly with the latest polling information. His approval rating was high in with Israelites and Egyptians.

I awoke and grabbed my Bible, opened it to Exodus and read how Moses did not succumb to the pressure of

Pharaoh, the Egyptians, or the Israelites, but instead kept looking for God, walking with God daily into whatever dangers arose.

I felt much better as I put my Bible down, but then I looked at a dollar bill and had to wonder...

I researched the Latin phrase over the pyramid, *Annuit Coeptis,* which means, "God blesses all our undertakings."

Throughout human history, we have always wanted to give God an address calling a Temple, Synagogue, or Sanctuary the House of The Lord, but The Lord has never seemed interested in our properties. It is neither Christian nor Jewish to put God in some Holy Place, but it is Greek. Zeus lived on the high mountain with the rest of the gods. That's our role model, to be the godly ruler of our own mountain or kingdom, while God keeps calling us to meet in some barren space as with Moses and Israel. Pharaoh is making slaves to build a pyramid, but God shows up in a shrub and speaks to Moses. Where is Moses to guide the Israelites once they leave Egypt? Out toward the desert to meet with God. God doesn't need the pyramid, the empire, the holy land or the sacred space. God is looking to encounter people.

Jesus never owned, acquired, or showed any interest in a tangible space he could occupy, instead, he was out meeting with God and people. The news of the cross is the same as the flaming shrub – if God can show up there, God can show up anywhere.

Pharaohs and Caesars base their kingdoms on square footage. For God, kingdom is about people with and between people. Which kingdom shapes our vision, our goals, our choices, and even our churches, Moses or Pharaoh, Jesus or Caesar? God calls us not to build a holy space, a holy building, or even a holy nation where we can schedule and structure our meetings with God. God calls us out into deserts, beyond structures, to encounter God in holy moments, sacred spaces in time, that can be anytime, anyplace, and in anyway that God chooses.

## Practice: Be Still to Know God

*We often fail in trying to understand God, not because we do not know how to extend our concepts far enough, but because we do not know how to begin close enough. To think of God is not to find God as an object in our minds, but to find ourselves in God.* Abraham Joshua Heschel

Frederick Buechner told of a period when he was struggling in his life and was reminded of his need for something and someone greater.

*I had the feeling that my life was disordered, directionless and somehow shabby, and a friend of*

*mine told me about an Episcopal monastery on the banks of the Hudson River, where there was a monk who he thought might be a good person for me to go see because he was a wise and good man. So, off I went in my car to that monastery, full of questions – there's a kind of wonderful divine comedy about all of this – and when I got there I found this particular monk, whom I'd been sent to see, had taken a vow of silence, and wasn't seeing anybody. I've felt since that the great value of those three days, in that monastery, was the silence. If I'd found the monk and asked my questions, he would have answered the questions and that wouldn't have solved anything. I've often thought if God had said to Job, "All right, I'll tell you why these terrible things happened. Here it is…" and given him six typewritten pages, it wouldn't have solved Job's problem either because, like me, he wasn't after answers. He was after something else, and what the silence said to me was, "Be still, and know that I am God." And that was another of these holy moments for me.*

Over the course of my quest to try to understand being still and being present, I have repeatedly recited to myself the well-known verse, "Be still and know that I am God." It is a wonderful phrase, but even more so when seen in its context. Here are excerpts from Psalm 46.

*God is our refuge and strength,*
   *a very present help in trouble.*

153

*Therefore we will not fear, though the earth should change,*
>*though the mountains shake in the heart of the sea;*
>*though its waters roar and foam,*
>*though the mountains tremble with its tumult.*

*Come, behold the works of the Lord;*
>*see what desolations he has brought on the earth.*
*He makes wars cease to the end of the earth;*
>*he breaks the bow, and shatters the spear;*
>*he burns the shields with fire.*

*"Be still, and know that I am God!*

The Psalm is full of praise of God, wonders at the works of God, thoughts of the nature of God, then, after all the verses about God, God breaks in and speaks, God demands, "Be still! Know that I am God."

To observe Christian worship from an objective place, one might think that God loves our music all played within the same few hours across the world on a single day of the week. It would be like listening to all your music at the same time. If it were really God's enjoyment we were after, wouldn't we coordinate our praise over the whole week? What God seeks is relationship, which happens in the moments of our lives. God seeks to know and be known. Would not God say the same to us? "Be still! Know that I am God. Stop talking so much about me and walk with me, live with me, know me."

## Practice: Make God Your Target Audience

I've spent a good bit of time with songwriters in Nashville. Like writers of books, a question they are commonly asked is, "Who is your target audience?" The question presents a challenge to any artist seeking the approval of others for a work that contains their personality and soul. However, the question does present a wonderful opportunity for reflection. Consider this image of a theater.

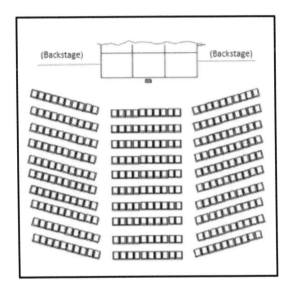

In the above theater, where would you place the following?

- Preacher
- Choir or Singers and Musicians
- Congregation
- God

The common response is to place the preacher, choir, and musicians on stage, the congregation in the audience, and God everywhere. We discuss worship as in any theater. My favorite complaint about a preacher came from my aunt, who is a Methodist, after they had just had their first Sunday with their 'new preacher' appointed to their church by the Bishop. She was very frustrated because he preached past 12:00 and committed an even greater transgression, he started talking about food. "Now David," she said to me, "you don't preach about fried chicken after 12:00 when everybody is hungry and thinking about lunch." She complained to me as if pastors were all part of a Union, and I might be able to take care of their long-winded preacher problem for her.

Soren Kierkegaard challenged our thinking of worship and said that we have the audience wrong. The congregation is not the audience. God is the audience. Those who gather for worship are on stage. The preacher, singers, and musicians are all backstage prompting the congregation. It is not our pleasure which is the final judge but God's. It is not whether or not we consider a service meaningful but whether God finds meaning in our service, in church and out, on holy days and every days.

Do you attend worship as a spectator? What about life? Who is the target audience of the moments of your life? Where is God in your personal theater? In the drama of your life, have you given God tickets or tried to bar the door? Does God find meaning in your worship? Does God find meaning in your life?

Eugene Peterson's *The Message* captures Jesus' challenge of making God our target audience. Here is his paraphrase of Matthew 6,

> *"Be especially careful when you are trying to be good so that you don't make a performance out of it. It might be good theater, but the God who made you won't be applauding.*
>
> [2-4] *"When you do something for someone else, don't call attention to yourself. You've seen them in action, I'm sure—'playactors' I call them—treating prayer meeting and street corner alike as a stage, acting compassionate as long as someone is watching, playing to the crowds. They get applause, true, but that's all they get. When you help someone out, don't think about how it looks. Just do it—quietly and unobtrusively. That is the way your God, who conceived you in love, working behind the scenes, helps you out.*

## Practice: Pray to an Audience of One

Somewhere in the recesses of my mind, I have a vague memory from my childhood when I prayed in a family or other group gathering. Someone, perhaps a sibling, snickered at the words I chose in my prayer. My mother, the ever protector, responded quickly, "He wasn't talking to you."

Jesus taught that prayer was never a public performance but a private one. Here are his words again from *The Message* and Matthew 6,

*⁵ "And when you come before God, don't turn that into a theatrical production either. All these people making a regular show out of their prayers, hoping for stardom! Do you think God sits in a box seat?*

*⁶ "Here's what I want you to do: Find a quiet, secluded place so you won't be tempted to role-play before God. Just be there as simply and honestly as you can manage. The focus will shift from you to God, and you will begin to sense his grace.*

Instead of doing a dance for the world, you do your dance for God, your audience of one, The One. Instead of proclaiming your righteousness, you seek alignment with the heart and desires of God. Paul Thorn offers a great image for when God is your target audience in a simple phrase in, *I Hope I'm Doing This Right,*

*Sometimes I wonder*
*How I made it this far*
*I've won some trophies*
*And I wear some ugly scars*
*Before I go to bed*
*I kneel and pray every night*
*I wonder if God's proud of me*
*I hope I'm doing this right*

*I know a lot of people*
*They appear to have it made*
*I battle with jealousy*
*Why can't I live that way?*
*Maybe they're just better than me*

158

*At playing the game of life*
*Maybe I need to change some things*
*I hope I'm doing this right*

*The more I learn the less I know*
*The more I change the more I grow*
*I pray the road I'm traveling on*
*Will lead me to the light*
*God, I hope I'm doing this right*

## Practice: Get into the Game

In this era of specialization, we have a professional for every area of our lives. If you want someone to fix your car, go see a mechanic. If you are feeling ill, go see a doctor. If you have a legal question, go see a lawyer. If you want someone to educate your children, take them to a school of teachers. If you have a Bible question, go see a pastor.

The result of such specialization is that we have turned church over to professionals. Like football teams, movies, restaurants, music celebrities, churches seek someone to draw a crowd. In comparison, as a measure of life in a church, "How many people were there on Sunday?" or "How many members does your church have?" Joseph Campbell said the worst mistake in the history of the church was when the priest turned from the altar, speaking to God on behalf of the people during worship, and turned toward the people speaking to them on behalf of God. Gauging by our behavior, if our actions were the only testimony to our faith, one might think Jesus called disciples to, "Come and watch me," instead of "Come and follow me." As a friend told me, we are fans of Jesus, not followers.

Imagine you came to Nashville and went with me to a Titans football game. Three running backs are injured and the coach comes into the stands and says to you, "We need you. Come play running back." Thinking about the size of these athletes, chances are, you'd reply, "I just came to watch."

Then we go to The Grand Ol' Opry for a show. The guitar player is sick. The organizer comes out into the stands and says, "We need you to come up on stage and play." Likely, you'd say, "But I just came to watch."

Then we go to a large church with a professional band and leaders, and during the service, Jesus walks up and taps you on the shoulder, and says, "Follow me."

You say, "But I just came to watch..." you wait for a moment, hoping Jesus will go away. You're regretting taking the seat on the aisle. It would have been much safer in the middle. Jesus says again, "Let's go."

"But I just came to worship," you say. "I love you. I believe. I've read your book. Big fans... me and my whole family..." You lift your hands and move them in the church version of "The Wave." Again, you're hoping he'll go away. Hoping he'll say, "Okay, have a nice day. See you in heaven." But he doesn't. Sure you might become so blinded by the crowd, unable to see anything without an affirmation, asking others, "Do you see what I see," not making a decision until everyone in your family agrees or all on your committee vote, "Aye!" But he keeps coming, calling you out, onto the stage, onto the field, into the moments of your life, becoming all God intends for you to be and become.

## Practice: Seek the Applause of Heaven

Faith is trusting your life has meaning, even though you'll likely not know it this side of heaven. Consider the writers of two of the most popular songs of all time: The 23rd Psalm and *Silent Night.* When the author of Psalm 23 was writing it, he (or she) didn't know it would last long after his (or her) trip through the valley of the shadow of death. There was no thought, "I'll bet one day this will be in The Bible." There was no Bible. When the author of *Silent Night* wrote that carol for guitar it was because the church organ broke, and they needed music for Christmas Eve. Is there a better irony than a song written about a silent night on an evening when the church organ wouldn't work?

Play your part. Sing the song God has for you. Live the divine narrative set before you letting your Christ-like character develop and your personal drama take care of itself. Through it all, listen for the applause of heaven.

## Practice: Seek the Divine, "Amen."

As a pastor, I have counseled many people who are frustrated because their lives did not develop along the story they wanted, hoped for, or expected. One of the more frustrating philosophical endeavors is to try to discover the meaning in some of the more meaningless times of our lives.

I heard of a songwriter in Nashville who dreamed of dying and going to heaven. In that glorious new life, he heard a band of angels playing and singing a song he had written. He told one of the angels with pride, "They are playing my song!"

The angel laughed and told him, "No, you were playing our song."

Faith is letting God have the story and living into God's story, fully developing your character the best you can. The question is not whether or not your life has meaning or your story makes sense or the plot is plain, but whether or not your life has meaning to God and makes sense to God. Instead of trying to have each part of your life make sense to the world, remember that the world is not your target audience, God is. Live in such a way to evoke the applause of heaven. Live in such a way to evoke a divine, "Amen!"

## Practice: Read the Bible Asking, "What Happens?"

When we read the Bible, we often approach with a linear sense of time. We think of ourselves as here and the Bible as a representation of God's past deeds, a record of back then when God did this and that. With this limited sense of time, we want to know, "Did it 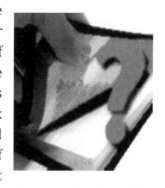 happen?" trying to come up with a simple fable-like morality and the singular definitive interpretation and implication. We may even profess, "God said it. I believe it. That settles it." When we read the Bible and place it in the past, we try to place God between the covers, instead of saying, "Here I am," and like Samuel, "Speak Lord, your servant is listening." We ask, "What happened?" We ask, "What did God do?" We ask, "What did God say?" The professionals answer as the congregations snooze, all is settled, the infants are pacified and return to their slumber. This once revealed and never revealing approach to The Word of God has the opposite effect of God's word and presence in the Bible. In Scripture, God's Word unsettles. No one goes back to sleep after God speaks.

Instead of asking, "What happened?" when we approach the Bible, a better question is, "What happens?" and instead of "What did God say?" ask, "What is God saying?"

For example, in Genesis 1, instead of trying to go backward wondering just how God created the world, Rabbi Heschel's approach is more biblical,

> *Creation... is not an act that happened once upon a time, once and for ever. The act of bringing the world into existence is a continuous process. God called the world into being, and that call goes on. There is this present moment because God is present. Every instant is an act of creation. A moment is not a terminal but a flash, a signal of Beginning. Time is perpetual innovation, a synonym for continuous creation...*
>
> *To witness the perpetual marvel of the world's coming into being is to sense the presence of the Giver in the given, to realize that the source of time is eternity, that the secret of being is the eternal within time.*

From the beginning, God encounters people in time. Limited by our place in time, we encounter God who is not. In the beginning, God created life and time and only in God can there be life and time. We are confined by time, God is not. When Moses encounters God at the bush that burns but is not consumed, besides the bush that doesn't burn up, God points toward God's place above time in what God says to Moses in Exodus 3. When God declares, "I am the God of your father, the God of Abraham, the God of Isaac, and the God of Jacob." God speaks not as if they were old friends from long ago but current companions. Even though Moses was limited by time God points to God's place beyond time. If God is still speaking, then God speaks through the Bible as God spoke through the bush, not in the past but in our presence. Better kick off your shoes, as Kierkegaard advised,

> When you read God's Word, you must constantly be saying to yourself, "It is talking to me, and about me.

## Practice: Read the Bible Asking, "Where's it Pointing?"

When it comes to the Bible, William Sloane Coffin observed, "We use the Bible like a drunk uses a lamppost, more for support than illumination." We would do well in our Bible reading to remember the ancient proverb, "When you see a finger pointing at the moon, don't look at the finger so that you miss all the heavenly glory."

Instead of reading the Bible looking for a point, the healthier way is to see where it points. Letting the Bible direct us toward God's work in the world is an approach Christians take at least once a year. Consider the famous

Christmas Carols you know by heart. I'll start a line and you finish it...

*O little town of Bethlehem, How still...*

*Silent night, holy night, All is calm...*

*Hark the herald angels sing...*

*Joy to the world, The Lord...*

In all those Christmas Carols, they have one thing in common – they point. They don't pointed backward, they point to now. They are all present tense.

*O little town of Bethlehem*
*How still we see thee lie.*

*Silent night, holy night*
*All is calm, all is bright.*

*Hark the herald angels sing*
*"Glory to the newborn King!*

*Joy to the world, the Lord is come!*

Not past tense ,"Joy to the world, the Lord has come." Not future, "Joy to the world the Lord will come" or "will come again." But "is come!" Now. "Go tell it on the mountain. Jesus Christ is born."

165

A healthier way to seek God in scriptures is to read it, like our Christmas carols, like the Magi letting God's stars, God's signs and wonders, point us toward Bethlehem and beyond.

## Practice: Read the Bible, Dreaming God's Dreams

*Prayer is frequently an inner vision, an intense dreaming for God – the reflection of the Divine intentions in the soul of people... To pray is to dream in league with God, to envision His holy visions.* Abraham Joshua Heschel

My connection with Etta Britt is so strong that at times I cannot tell if she is singing my sermons or if I'm preaching her songs.

We started The Moment just after Etta had released her first cd, *Out of The Shadows*. The disc contains a song that has become my theme. The song is, *I Believe*,

*It's just a matter of time,*
*we're gonna wake up to find.*
*This world is moving so fast*
*every moment, make it last.*

*When you give hope then you'll see,*
*love is all we need to believe.*
*A touch of a hand, one smile*
*make someone 's life worthwhile*

*I believe...*

*A little bit of faith goes a long long way,*
*a change of heart, there's a better day*
*Let's come together, it's you and me,*
*faith, hope, and love is all we'll need*

*I believe...*
*Time will come when we'll understand*
*what it means to help someone.*
*There will come a day*
*we'll walk hand in hand,*
*and we're gonna shine in the light*
*of the wonderful sun!*

On September 11th, while preparing for a congregation to gather in worship as an act of faith and defiance of terrorism, Etta called me and said, "I have a song." She shared a vision for the world I believe God's people are called to live into reality. The song is, *Peace Stories* by George McCorkle, Bruce Birch, and Vip Vipperman,

*Last night I had a beautiful dream*
*A young boy sat on his Grandpa's knee*
*And the old man told a story of*
*how the world became one*
*When the armies of all nations*
*laid down their guns.*

*Maybe one day we'll all be telling peace stories*
*To our children, God willin', all over the earth*
*Maybe one day the world will live in Love's glory*
*And war will be a forgotten word*

*Peace stories are all that will be heard.*

*Old soldiers won't be showing their scars*
*When the battles are all over*
*they'll be sharing their hearts*
*Handing down wisdom and not hatred or fear*
*There will be the sound of laughter,*
*not the silence of tears.*

Instead of placing God's Kingdom mentally in some far off future, pray for God's Kingdom – Now! Pray this practice by beginning each day by praying, "Thy Kingdom come – Today!" Here is a version of The Lord's Prayer I use to remind me to pray for God's dreams to become my dreams.

*Father, in heaven,*
*Hallowed is Your Name.*

*Your kingdom NOW.*
*Your will NOW.*
*in me as in heaven,*
*in my home as in heaven,*
*on earth as in heaven,*
*in me as in You.*
*NOW, not tomorrow,*
*TODAY, not later*
*NOW!*

## Practice: Read the Bible Asking, "What do I do?"

One of the best structures I found in preparing a sermon is three simple questions, "What?" "So what?" and "Now what?" Those are also helpful questions in reading the Bible, especially remembering to end with, "Now what?"

The debates over the Bible are never ceasing with countless commentaries. As the author of Ecclesiastes warned, "The writing of books is endless and wearying to the soul."

However, what God requires does not require volumes but lifetimes. The prophet Micah asked, "What does the Lord require of us?" The answer is memorable, even singable, "Seek justice. Love kindness. Walk humbly with your God." Jesus summed up the law and prophets when asked what God wants from us. "To love God with all that we are, and to love our neighbors in the same way we love ourselves."

Once we read those commands and focus on them, our emphasis changes from past to present, principles to practices, and from religion to relationships.

## Practice: Expect New Beginnings

When I pick up a book, I pay close attention to the first lines. I think if an author wants to grab me, they should start at the beginning. Here are a few of the classics:

*Call me Ishmael.* Herman Melville, *Moby Dick*

*Happy families are all alike; every unhappy family is unhappy in its own way.* Leo Tolstoy, *Anna Karenina*

*All children, except one, grow up.* J.M. Barrie, *Peter Pan.*

*It was a bright, cold day in April, and the clocks were striking thirteen.* George Orwell, *1984*.

In the Bible, there is a library's worth of first lines, sixty-six in all. The classic is from Genesis, *In the beginning, God created...* Thought to be the oldest gospel, Mark reflects Genesis in his message about Jesus starting with, *This (is just) the beginning of the good news of Jesus the Christ...* (my emphasis added). The original ending of Mark has Easter with the women going to the tomb and seeing an angel who tells them, *Don't be afraid. You're looking in this tomb for Jesus of Nazareth, who was crucified, but he's not here... He's going ahead of you, into Galilee...* They go away afraid, and that's it. Mark's original ending was not left unscathed. Several other endings were added including a part about handling snakes. These additions miss Mark's purpose -- to let us know that the life, death, and resurrection of Jesus was, *just the beginning.* For Mark, Jesus was out of the tomb and off the page and in the world. We can run home like the women afraid, or we can go ahead, out into the world as the angel advises, looking for the one who is already out there, going ahead of us.

Whether in search of a haunting great white whale, whether your family is happy or not, whether you are struggling unsuccessfully to not grow up like Peter Pan, or even if your clock is striking 13 and you're losing whatever illusions you held onto before, Mark wants you to know, Jesus is out there. Look for him. Out of the tomb. Off the page. In the world.

## Practice: Expect the Miraculous

There is a simple difference between magic and miracle. Magic has a formula, an incantation, and produces a desired result. Churches often offer magical formulas: six ways to a happy marriage, four ways to a better relationship with God, three steps to effective prayer, while promising in each path you will achieve your desired goals. Here is a simple formula for homes and churches with great results: do not spend more than you make, keep income greater than expenses. Managing money in homes and churches is largely about managing anxiety. If you can save 10% and give away 10%, then your life will be happier and less stressful.

While saving 10% and giving away 10% is a simple formula, numbers in the miraculous life of Jesus are far different. They look like this: 5 loaves and 2 fish to feed 5,000; 2 coins a widow gave in the Temple which Jesus said were more than the thousands others gave; 200 miles (the farthest Jesus traveled from his boyhood home); 3 years of ministry; 12 disciples; and 1 life which changed the world.

Miracles are far different from magic. In miracles, there is no formula; they are never identical: they come in ways you don't expect; and they probably will scare the hell out of you. Remember that on the first Easter, when the attendees saw the empty tomb they ran in fear.

While we keep trying to figure out how to make the Bible, church, and God work for us, God is trying to call us out to join God in the miraculous kingdom vision God has planned for the world. Moments offer no magic formula, but inside moments, miracles abound for those present to see them as the wise Sophia advised,

> *"Sophia, why do you pray?" asked the skeptic. "Do you pray to make the sun come up?"*
>
> *"No," replied Sophia, "I pray so that when the sun comes up I will be awake to see it."*

Do not pray to get God to work for you, pray so that you may find yourself alive in the warmth, light, and wonderful workings of God in the moments of your life and the world.

## Practice: Expect Jesus to Kick in Your Door

When I was younger, there was an evangelism program called, *I Found It,* complete with celebrities, booklets, and bumper stickers. One of the messages of the advertising campaign used the image from Revelation 3 with Jesus standing at my door and

knocking, promising if I will just let him in, he will come in and be my friend.

As an adult, in Russia, on a trip I did not select as much as was sent, I was in the home of one of my new friends who had an almost life-size framed picture of Jesus standing at the door and knocking. "Do you know this passage?" he asked. "Yes," I said, "but in my life, I feel more like Jesus doesn't knock and wait hoping I'll open it, but my experience with Jesus is that he kicks it in." Even after translated by another in Russian, he did not seem to understand. I wish I had Gordon Kennedy with me to help explain. He has a marvelous way of singing about Jesus in songs like, *Can't Shake Jesus,*

> *naked, alone, cold cobblestones*
> *they beat Him until the blood ran*
> *they brought Him to die, on a cross, up on-high*
> *with spikes through His feet and His hands*
>
> *a crown of thorns on His brow, His eye on the crowds*
> *all of God's daughters and sons*
> *they're spitting on Him, cursing at Him*
> *"Forgive them for what they have done...*
> *you can use Him, abuse Him, mock and accuse Him*
> *sell Him out for thirty pieces*
> *betray Him, slay Him, do the devil's mayhem*
> *but you can't shake Jesus*
>
> *well I've had my bouts, questions and doubts*
> *you know there are those who deceive*
> *I've tried to resist, escape and dismiss*
> *but there's one who's shadowing me*

*I can lose my religion, break with tradition*
*say I'll hold out till Hell freezes*
*I can test Him, try Him, but I just can't deny Him*
*no, I can't shake Jesus*

Here is my promise. Run if you want. Hide if you can. I don't see it going well for you. If he's after you, he'll find you. You can't shake him. A warning Edith Lovejoy Pierce captured in her poem, *Drum Major for a Dream,*

> *Above the shouts and the shots,*
> *The roaring flames and the siren's blare,*
> *Listen for the stilled voice of the man*
> *Who is no longer there.*
> *Above the tramping of the endless line*
> *Of marches along the street,*
> *Listen for the silent step*
> *of the dead man's invisible feet.*
> *Lock doors, put troops at the gate,*
> *Guard the legislative halls*
> *But tremble when the dead man comes,*
> *Whose spirit walks through walls.*

## Practice: Be Christ's Contemporary

Churches today post advertisements for their worship services as Traditional or Contemporary. Soren Kierkegaard said long ago that what the world needed was not Contemporary Worship but Contemporary Christians. Here is my paraphrase of a section from Kierkegaard's *Practices in Christianity.* I used translations by Robert Bretall and Charles Bellinger.

*If becoming a Christian is expressed as anything other than becoming Christ's contemporary in the present, all the talk is nonsense, self-deception, and conceit. For in relation to the absolute, there is only one tense: the present tense.*

*The three, or seven, or fifteen, or eighteen hundred years which have elapsed since his death do not make the least difference one way or the other. They neither change him, nor reveal, either, who he was. Christ is no simple historical figure that once was and can be reflected upon backward. Historic Christianity is sheer moonshine or muddle-headedness. For those true Christians who in every generation live a life contemporaneous with Christ have no real connection with previous generations of Christianity. They are past. Christ is not. Christ is present. Christ is now. Christ is contemporary and his followers live contemporary with Christ as Christ's companions, Christ's followers, and Christ's disciples.*

## Practice: Seek, Don't Get Stuck

I grew up in a textile mill neighborhood in South Carolina where the language we spoke was far from Kierkegaard's prose, yet it had a poetic cadence and was often quite colorful. Returning to my roots, here is my retelling of Saul's conversion in Acts chapter nine.

There once a fellow named Saul. He was going about, hounding all of Jesus' followers in the early church, throwing them in jail as the lawbreakers he thought they were. He'd even promote a lynching or stoning if there wasn't a prison close by. Saul believed in God, and in a way that the confident often are, he was certain he was carrying out God's will by preserving the right, the true, the holy tradition.

The risen Jesus was getting tired of Saul's shenanigans. While on the road to a place called Damascus, Jesus caught up with Saul and smacked him to the ground. Jesus appeared in a blinding light, the kind of light you go toward when you're dying but don't want to see until then. Then Jesus spoke, "Saul, what the hell are you doing? Why are you being such a pain in my backside?"

Saul didn't have any idea who would smack him down in such a way and then accuse him of doing wrong when he was so sure he had been in the right persecuting all of the followers of Jesus and shutting that movement down before it could get going good.

Saul asked, "Who is this?"

To Saul's surprise, the voice replied as if Saul should have known, "It's me, Jesus."

Saul thought what all of us think when we were so sure we were right and got caught in the wrong facing the biggest butt whooping we've ever had, 'Oh, #####!'

Jesus changed Saul's name to Paul. Apparently, Saul was only Saul for the moment. Paul then traveled around much of the known world looking for Jesus everywhere he went. As the saying goes, surprise me once, shame on you, but surprise me twice, shame on me. Paul wasn't going to let Jesus spook him like that again. Along Paul's divine game of hide and seek with Jesus, he started new church communities and wrote much of the New

Testament though he only thought he was writing letters at the time.

For much of this same era, Peter, who had spent a significant amount of time with Jesus before and after Easter, was going nowhere. He got stuck in Jerusalem trying to keep everyone together. The resurrected Jesus had instructed Peter and the other disciples to, "Go into all the world," and promised, "I'll be with you." Peter didn't seem to understand that in Jesus' Godly way, he and the others had been tagged and were it, expected to continue the game and look for Jesus. Instead, Peter served the early church by working in conflict management. He sat on several committees. The most controversial was the one that not only debated what kinds of foods Jesus' followers had to eat but more significantly was what accoutrements the genitals of Gentiles had to have before becoming card carrying church club members. Peter sought a consensus over circumcision, though even today Gentile Christian male babies are still being circumcised hoping to pacify first century Jews. While Paul was struck down trying to tear the church apart, Peter got stuck trying to keep it all together hoping the right policy would do it. The tragedy here is even greater when considering that, among the disciples, Peter was the brave one.

# Practice: Church

What time is church?

The best answer is, "Now."

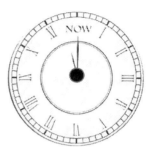

When we first started meeting for worship in The Moment, we took up an offering. Instead of passing a plate, we asked people to come forward. The physical movement was to help take us out of the spectator role of an audience and into the place of participants. It also served as an example of what we are called to do as followers of Jesus, step out into the world.

While getting up and coming forward to give an offering is the norm in some traditions, it was not in ours. Whether in a sanctuary or a bar, whether the person was six or sixty, if called to come forward for the offering, everyone would look around and wait for one thing to happen before they would move. Someone had to go first. In a crowd of five or five hundred, if something new is started, people will look for someone to go first before they move. For our offerings, usually a mother would push her child into the aisle. As soon as the child would venture out, then everyone would follow. It always took the one.

Followers of Jesus are called to be the one, to step first, to cross the distances that separate us, to try the miraculous, to sing the song that needs to be sung or speak the words that need to be spoken. We stopped taking a collection at The Moment because we wanted to change the message. Better than, "Give to The Moment," or "We need your offerings," we reminded each other, "Our lives are our offerings. We each have parts to play in God's story and the story is happening now." If church is over when worship ends, then we leave and blend back into our crowds where no one is the one, no one is called out, where we all wait for someone to go 1st, 2nd, 3rd, 4th…. However, if church begins when worship finishes, if church is our way in the world, then one life, one moment, one encounter, one miracle at a time, the world will change. When God's people step out person by person with Jesus' life as our way in the world, then the world will be transformed. The kingdom of God will become a reality. Jesus never asked for 10% but 100%, or as my coaches used to say, "I want 110%!"

At some point in Jerusalem, Peter wakes to his unconscious life in committee and steps back out in the world. He remembers being with Jesus in his younger days and how more than anything he wanted to be with Jesus regardless of the risk.

In Matthew 14, Jesus sent the disciples out into a storm then came walking to them on water. The disciples, Peter included, all wanted to be with Jesus. The difference between Peter and the other eleven was simple, while they wanted to be with Jesus in their sanctuary, their safe place, their boat, Peter wanted to be with Jesus in that moment, even in the storm, even if it took a miracle to get to him. Foolish? Yes. Crazy? Yes. Risky? Of course. Did he fail? Yes. Did he fall? Yes. But his goal was to be with Jesus in every moment, in the craft or on the surf, in the boat or in the storm, wherever Jesus was, that's where he wanted to be.

When Jesus and Peter got into the boat, the other disciples proclaimed, "Truly you are the Son of God," they believed. Peter trusted. They had the creed. Peter had faith.

# About the Author

David Jones is a pastor and author of the following:

*Out of The Crowd*

*Enough!*

*The Psychology of Jesus:*

*Jesus Zens You*

*Moses and Mickey Mouse:*

*For the Love of Sophia*

*Going Nuts!* (Fiction)

*The Way and The Word*
*The Tao of Jesus*

*Absurdus We Pray*

*Prayer Primer*

For more information on these books,
go to: www.davidjonespub.com

Contact David at: davidjonespub@outlook.com.

# The Moment Music

*I Believe* and *Quiet House* are on Etta Britt's *Out Of The Shadows. Can't Impress Jesus* has yet to be recorded. Find out more about Etta's music at *ettabritt.com* including her new cd of Delbert McClinton's music – *Etta Does Delbert.*

*Reason to Try* and *I Was a Burden* are on Danny Flower's *Tools For The Soul.*

*Words Won't Come* by Carol Warren and Dale Whitehead has yet to be recorded. Other songs of theirs are on *Legacy.*

*Let It Go* is on The McCrary Sisters' *All The Way.*

*Let it Go* and *God Speaks to Me Through You* are on Travis Meadows' *Killing Uncle Buzzy.*

A comprehensive list of Paul Thorn's recordings including all the songs referenced can be found at *paulthorn.com*

Made in the USA
Columbia, SC
17 June 2019